Debra LaFave
A Crown of Beauty for Ashes

A BIOGRAPHY OF THE LIFE OF
DEBRA JEAN BEASLEY

BY

JOE ZUNIGA

the Peppertree Press
Sarasota, Florida

The statements, opinions and data contained in this publication is solely that of the individual author and not of the publisher, the Peppertree Press.
Peppertree Press is not responsible for the content in this book.
Zuniga Marketing, Inc. takes full responsibility.

Copyright © Joe Zuniga, 2016

All rights reserved. Published by the Peppertree Press, LLC.
The Peppertree Press and associated logos are trademarks of the Peppertree Press, LLC.

No part of this publication may be reproduced, stored in a retrieval system, transmitted in any form or by any means, electronic, mechanical, photocopying, recording, or otherwise, without prior written permission of the publisher and author/illustrator.
Graphic design by Rebecca Barbier.

For information regarding permission,
call 941-922-2662 or contact us at our website:
www.peppertreepublishing.com or write to:
the Peppertree Press, LLC.
Attention: Publisher
1269 First Street, Suite 7
Sarasota, Florida 34236

ISBN: 978-1-61493-469-1
Library of Congress Number: 2016913530
Printed September 2016

In memory of, my inspiration, my queen, my mother, Maria G. Zuniga!

Contents

PROLOGUE	1
CHILDHOOD	3
EARLY SEXUAL EXPOSURE & ADOLESENCE	10
UNIVERSITY OF SOUTH FLORIDA	25
BUTTERFLIES	37
BECOMING A SEXUAL OFFENDER	57
AFTER THE ARREST	78
THERAPY	87
EPILOGUE: LIFE EVER AFTER	98
ABOUT THE AUTHOR	103

PROLOGUE

The purpose of this book is not to explain, shame, or hurt; in fact, it's quite the opposite. Debra Jean Beasley LaFave is known to the world as a beautiful monster, a seductive pervert, a lovely wrecker of lives. How difficult must it be to live in a world that views you in such extreme polarities? When the media portrays someone as a sex object, or worse as a monster, it is easy to forget that that person developed over time. The story of "now" overshadows the story of "then." It is only when the dust has settled and the news outlets are looking for ways to boost their ratings that the backstory is investigated and considered. But sometimes I wonder, what truly is more interesting – what has happened, or why it has happened and how has it come to this?

I came to know Debra, whom will henceforth be referred to as Debbie, through family. My sister, Cris Zuniga Meza, worked with Debbie at a community health center for about 3 years. Debbie previously worked as a waitress with Cris' son at Danny Boy's, a local restaurant. When hired at the Medical Clinic, Debbie worked as an administrative assistant in the finance department. The CEO, Mr. Smith, lived in Ruskin and had known Debbie for a long time. He gave her a second chance. Rumors started spreading through the facilities that Debra LaFave was going to work there. Debbie was really nice, and quite funny. Cris and Debbie immediately became friends. I would sometimes visit my sister at work, bring her lunch or just stop by to visit. She introduced me to Debbie.

This is Debbie's story, though she has privileged me with sharing it. Yes, I do say privileged because though many may disagree, I find her to be intriguing and dynamic. It is not for me to judge a man or woman based on their past. I found that Debbie's story resonated with my own. I was walked life down the wrong path and ended up in prison. People can judge me, and often do, for my past; but since that time I have made immense personal changes and have grown immeasurably. Looking back, I can see the transformation that I have made and just how far I have come from the troubled youth of my past. Learning about who Debbie is now, looking back on her life and all that it entails, I cannot help but feel moved by and connected to her. Her tale is truly one of transformation.

For privacy, many names in this text have been altered. Again, I am in no way attempting to emotionally hurt any of those who may have been affected by the events in Debbie's life. Much of what will be shared throughout this text is very sensitive to the parties involved, including Debbie, and all information will be treated with the utmost sensitivity and respect.

Joe Zuniga

CHILDHOOD

Debra Jean Beasley was born on August 28, 1980 to Larry and Joyce Beasley. She was named Debra after an attractive actress, and given the middle name, Jean, after her grandmother – though it should be noted that for the majority of her life, she has been called, Debbie. Additionally, Larry and Joyce had one older daughter, Angela Beasley, born October 10, 1976. The Beasley family lived in a small house on 12th Street in Ruskin, Florida – a small town of roughly 5,000 people at the time of Debbie's birth.

Small town life is often full of charm, but too often darkness rests beneath the surface. Larry worked as a coal and fuel analyst for Tampa Electric. Joyce worked in banking, but attended cosmetology school at night while Angie and Debbie were young. Her dream was to become a hairdresser, and that sometimes meant sacrificing time with her family to go to school and make that happen.

Despite this, Joyce loved her daughters greatly. Debbie was easy to love. She was a beautiful blue eyed, blonde haired little bundle of joy. Parents will always tell you they love their children equally, but Debbie believes that her father favored her sister, Angie, and her mother favored her. Larry would often spend time fishing with Angie while Debbie helped Joyce in the kitchen.

Joyce treated the girls differently. Debbie, the beautiful baby, remained just that into her early childhood – the baby. Angie loved to take care of her sister, often calling Debbie her "doll." Strangers often gawked at Debbie as if she were a doll as well. Her physical beauty astounded all those who came into contact with her. They were drawn to her. Debbie clung to her mother often, fearful of any separation from her. Joyce would wrap Debbie in a warm embrace, filling her baby with love.

Of the two, Joyce was the affectionate parent. Larry was relatively cold. Some might describe him as a non-parent. He rarely showed affection towards the girls. Similarly, if Angie or Debbie misbehaved, he would show his disapproval by withdrawing from them further. Like children do, Debbie often would not pick up her toys. Joyce would take her by the arm over to the toys and tell her to put them away while Larry lay on the floor watching television. Joyce was the primary disciplinarian for the girls as well. They were rarely spanked; instead they were corrected verbally.

Larry was quick to anger. He had a distinct distain when something did not go according to the way he liked – and what he liked was control. Though he often removed himself emotionally from Debbie and her sister, Joyce received the brunt of his outbursts. In a small house, voices travel through thin walls. Debbie often heard her father yelling, cursing at her mother. Many times it was a result of something Debbie had done. Larry never confronted or instructed Debbie as she grew, but made it very clear to Joyce when she fell short of his expectations. She solemnly endured his rage, usually apologizing at the conclusion.

Childhood

Debbie was never fearful of her father. His yelling at her was normal in her innocent eyes. As a young girl, it's easy to imagine wishing for your father's approval, especially when he rarely gave it. Debbie tried and tried to "be good" so Larry would warm up to her, love her. But try as she might, she failed over and over again. Each time chipping away at the foundation of their relationship until it would eventually be on the verge of crumbling all together. To this day, she can count on her hands the number of times Larry initiated a hug or an, "I love you." In many ways, Debbie feels that her relationship with her father throughout her childhood shaped her future relationships. She continued to be attention seeking, especially with men. She sought out their approval and often felt the need to perform for others to gain their love and affection.

Joyce was able to fill the void Larry left in Debbie's heart. Where Larry's emotional well was dry, Joyce's overflowed in compensation. She was slow to anger, quick to console and provide. Like good mothers do, she tucked Debbie in to bed at night, kissed away her nightmares and tears, and tended to her while she was sick.

At an early age, Debbie became extremely attached to her mother and could not let go of this attachment. At only four months old, Debbie would cry if anyone tried to take her from her mother's arms. Joyce could not be in the room with Debbie while someone else held her. In some of her earliest memories, Debbie remembers clinging to her mother's leg every morning when Joyce tried to drop her off at preschool. Debbie would scream and cry until a teacher came and pealed her from Joyce's leg. She cried ceaselessly throughout the day, not earning a sticker for good behavior. Though this sort of separation anxiety is typical in some children, the duration and intensity of Debbie's anxious outbursts were not.

The transition of going to school and separating from her mother eased once Debbie entered Kindergarten at Ruskin Elementary. Her teacher was soft spoken and kind, and treated each child as though they were her own. Debbie felt safe here. She never anticipated that school would become a place to be hurt.

Debbie surprisingly didn't have many friends. She was very shy and tended to stay within her comfort zone. Those she called friends were her cousin, Samantha, and Emily, a girl she had known since preschool. Debbie and her friends loved to play "house" and "school" with her Barbie dolls. Her bedroom was full of dolls, clothes, shoes, and even a Barbie townhouse. She would sit and play for hours with her dolls. She always wanted to be a teacher. She would line all her dolls in a row and teach them how to read. Debbie didn't often go outside, because her parents (her mother most likely) were extremely protective and cautious with her, likely because her beauty attracted the attention of many, including potential predators. Debbie, however, was completely content playing in her imaginary world.

She loved school. Her parents always thought she was very bright, and up until about fourth grade, Debbie excelled. She was the "teacher's pet," well regarded by the adults. She was obedient, cooperative, and eager to help in any way. She enjoyed their attention and approval. She enjoyed learning. Debbie treated her schoolwork like treasure, re-doing and perfecting it before handing it in. No matter what the situation, Debbie always put forth her full effort. But in fourth grade, she started to notice changes at school. Her teachers didn't need her help as much anymore, and when they did, there were several other girls in the classroom willing to step in. Debbie felt that she started to fade into the background. Additionally, she began to have a difficult time concentrating in class. Her parents were able to offer only limited support in this area, so Debbie was left to manage it on her own. She fairly consistently brought home A's on her report cards, but earned B's on many assignments. She felt that her parents expected her to make A's because she was their smart child. Angie didn't do nearly as well in school. Joyce later told Debbie that it was Debbie who put the most pressure on herself to excel academically. A's were the expectation; B's were acceptable; C's were out of the question. Debbie worked hard to earn the grades she did. They were not handed to her. Debbie's favorite subject was English. She never wavered in her desire to teach. Though she didn't know what she wanted to teach at the time, she constantly reminded herself of the importance of school and an education.

Religion was not directly spoken about in the Beasley home, though it did play a role in Debbie's upbringing. The family – well, the girls – semi regularly attended Southside Baptist Church of Sun City. Both Angie and Debbie were baptized there. It was not until the girls were older that Debbie's aunt began taking she and Angie to church regularly. She would pick up the girls Wednesdays and Sundays for church. She guided Debbie spiritually.

Call it what you will, drama or trauma, but Debbie's life was not in short supply of these defining moments. Debbie's maternal grandmother, whom she was close with, passed away when Debbie was four years old. Around the age of five, Debbie began to develop a close relationship with an elderly neighbor, Mr. Martin. He was a gentle, white-haired man who lived just a few houses down from the Beasleys. Debbie and her mother would often visit him at his house and spend time chatting or playing games with him in his backyard. In his last few weeks of life, Debbie brought him watermelon to eat. It was the summer before kindergarten for Debbie, and she sweetly wanted to take some to her favorite neighbor. Mr. Martin smiled and thanked her for the delicious treat in the Florida heat. He ate a few pieces while Debbie smiled at him. Suddenly, he started coughing and gasping for air. His hand shakily drummed against his chest. Debbie's eyes were wide with fear. Mr. Martin was able to regain his composure, but Debbie had seen too much. Her eyes filled with tears and she ran home to her mother.

It was during this same time in her life that Debbie began to have panic attacks and mysophobia (fear of germs). She became exceedingly upset if she believed someone was going to vomit. She would cover her ears tightly and start to cry. She would repeatedly need to be reassured that it was okay, and that the person was going to be fine, and was not in life-threatening danger. Debbie often needed her mother to comfort her in these situations. On one occasion, Joyce was asked to babysit a close friend's three-year-old daughter. Unfortunately, she contracted the flu and had been throwing up prior to being dropped off at the Beasley home. Debbie was so angry with her mother for agreeing to watch the sick child, and equally as angry at the child's mother for having the audacity of bringing her to their home, that she stormed out of the house because she couldn't stand to be there.

At Debbie's eighth birthday, her cousin, Samantha, was in a terrible car accident. The car erupted in flames and Samantha was left with 3rd degree burns that covered her entire body. While the burns healed, she was left a paraplegic for the rest of her life. Numerous times the family was told that she would not live. Debbie was compelled to join her mother in visiting Samantha while she was hospitalized. Samantha and her family were on the way to Debbie's party when the accident occurred. Debbie felt tremendous guilt about this, often saying that Sam should have been at the party.

When Debbie was a young teen, her sister, Angie, suffered a serious gunshot accident as well. She was hospitalized for 12 days – five of which she spent in intensive care. Debbie's mother stayed with Angie the entire time she was hospitalized, and Debbie stayed at home with her father and visited Angie in the evenings. Angie recovered, but Debbie's anxiety did not.

EARLY SEXUAL EXPOSURE & ADOLESENCE

The "birds and the bees" is one conversation most parents dread discussing with their children and accordingly put it off for as long as possible. Sex was never discussed in the Beasley household. Maybe it should have been. Children who don't learn about sex and sexual exploration within their home will learn about it eventually.

When Debbie was about 10 or 11 years old, she went over to her friend Sandy's house. At some point during the course of the visit, Sandy said she was watching the Playboy channel and she saw a lady touching herself. Debbie had no idea what she was talking about, so Sandy pulled up her skirt and spread her legs out, facing Debbie. Debbie watched as Sandy moved her fingers in a circular motion on top of her pink underwear. She told Debbie that her underwear would get wet, but it was no big deal and told Debbie to try it. She was uncomfortable, but gingerly began to rub her panties. It did feel good, but Debbie still thought it was strange.

Debbie often spent the night at Sandy's house, like many children love to do with friends. Sandy's father was a good friend of Larry's. Adults are trusting of their adult friends to care for their children; and, let's face it, sometimes adults just need a break from their own kids. Whatever was the case for Joyce and Larry, they felt comfortable in sending Debbie to have sleepovers at Sandy's house. One night was different. Debbie remembers very little about the exact happenings of that night, but believes now that Sandy's father could very well have fondled her in his daughter's room while they slept.

It's common for victims of abuse to repress their memories of the abuse, and in Debbie's case, this is likely what happened. She now has vivid flashbacks to this moment, but cannot verify whether or not they are real.

The first boy she dated was Nick Carter – and, yes, that is *the* Nick Carter, as in the (future) Backstreet Boy. The pair dated for nearly a year and a half before it ended in a cheating scandal. Well, all right, a teenage boy cheating on his girlfriend isn't unheard of, but Debbie was very much devastated about it. What's more is that the end of this relationship didn't just mean a split from a longtime boyfriend; it was the end of a potential singing career. For as lovely was Debbie's face, so was her voice. While the two were an item, Nick's manager was working with Debbie – having her learn a song that he was considering having her record – but as soon as the split, so did the manager and any hope of becoming a professional singer.

Debbie's first sexual experience occurred at the tender age of 13. She was in middle school and developed a crush on a boy named, Juan. He was 15 years old, over-aged due to being held back twice. Juan was taken with Debbie's beauty, and she liked the attention he gave her. Joyce disapproved of the coupling, and told Debbie not to see him. She even called Juan herself after finding an explicit note he had written to Debbie in Debbie's room. Joyce told him to stay away from her daughter, and Debbie was not allowed to go anywhere alone except for youth group. But her warnings fell upon the deaf hears of her teenage daughter.

After a few months of dating and doing little more than kissing and touching, Debbie's rose-colored romance came to a crash. Valentine's day 1994 proved to be one of the most influential in her young life. She was babysitting for a couple in her neighborhood while they when out to dinner and a movie. She often babysat for this family. She enjoyed babysitting because it gave her a sense of confidence and responsibility. The children she watched loved her too. She had accepted the job because she and Juan hadn't made any plans themselves, but he knew where Debbie was that night. Around eight o'clock she heard a knock at the door.

She hesitantly opened the front door. She knew his face, but didn't read his intentions. The baby, Christopher, was banging on his piano in the living room. In his hands Juan held two green carnations, which she found particularly odd since it was Valentine's Day. In the primal part of her young mind, she felt apprehensive. The hairs on the back of her neck raised and she felt goose bumps spread down her arms. Not fully understanding her body's reactions she accepted the flowers and invited him into the house. That was the *only* invitation he received from Debbie.

Debbie was thirteen years old, babysitting on Valentine's Day. She never expected for this night to shape her entire future, her entire young adult development; but it would.

He looked around the house as Debbie closed the door behind him.

Early Sexual Exposure & Adolesence

"So, what?" he said. "No present for me?"

Debbie flushed. She didn't have anything for him and fumbled for the words to express her apologies and embarrassment.

"I don't have anything," she stuttered.

His eyes devoured her. He bit his lower lip and chuckled as he shook his head and pulled Debbie against him. "Oh, but you do have something to give me!" he smoothly whispered in her ear as he slid is fingers around the waistline of her jeans toward her navel. His breath smelled of cigarette smoke and booze. Again, every hair on her body stood on end and goose bumps covered her skin.

Not that! She thought desperately. She had barely even been to second base. She pushed his hand away from her and said, "No." The baby continued to play amicably on his piano in the living room. She didn't want to draw attention to herself, though perhaps if she had…

"Oh, come on, Deb. You know you want it." With every step she took back, he matched it forward. He shadowed her every move touching her arms, her chest, her neck. She backed away into another room, all the while telling him no, telling him to stop. She didn't want this.

She entered the room and turned to close the door, but he was there. His motions were so quick it stunned her. He caught her wrist in his left hand, and pawed at her shirt with the right. He pulled her against his body and sucked her neck. Her body went numb, like he was draining her of life. He pulled off her shirt and then her bra. She tried to cover her barely developed breasts, embarrassed and vulnerable. Guilt flooded her young body. This dark, heavy guilt would haunt her for years to come.

Debbie's memories of this horrific night are blurred. Her doctors say this is a normal defense mechanism for rape victims.

Tears welled in her blue eyes and she wondered whether she should fight him. He became more eager, hungrier with each passing second. Debbie stood frozen as he slipped her jeans down. Fully exposed, Debbie cried meekly to him, "Please, stop. Please, don't." Tears rolled down her cheeks. Her words fell on deaf ears.

He turned her over, holding her head down. She stared at the tarnished, white carpet as he forced himself into her. At thirteen years old, Debbie had her innocence ripped from her, and with it, part of her soul.

The pain was indescribable. There was no love, no tenderness, only pain. She cried ceaselessly and couldn't tell if she was crying because of the pain or because of what was happening to her. He pumped himself in and out of her, but became frustrated when he wasn't able to finish.

He picked her up, turned her around, and pushed her head down into his lap. "This should make it feel better," he said – whether to himself or to Debbie, she was unsure. She knew he was expecting her to open her mouth for him, but she turned her tear stained face away, pleading with him to stop. He tried to redirect her towards him to satisfy his urges. Her lips ran against him, but she could not perform the act he so desired.

Rage overtook him. He yanked Debbie from the floor and rammed himself inside her again and again. Debbie only remembers crying and wishing it would end.

As soon as he finished, he flew out the door, leaving Debbie naked and alone on the floor. She pulled herself into a tight ball and tried to compose herself. *I have to get back to the baby*, she thought. She found her clothes, which had been tossed carelessly around the room. She gingerly stepped into her jeans, wincing at the pain. Redressed she found the baby, ironically still banging away with his toys, happy as ever.

The doorbell startled her, and she took the child's hand as she walked towards the front of the house. She peeked out of the window beside the door. *It's him.* He appeared manic.

"Get rid of the condom!" he shouted through the glass. *Condom?* His fist pounded against the door, rattling the frame. "Get rid of it!"

Where was the condom? She walked quickly back to the room where she had just been violated. She fell to her hands and knees, crawling on the floor searching for the piece of evidence, all the while shaking out visions, ghosts of what had happened minutes before. There, lying under a table was the unused condom. This was the first time Debbie had ever touched a condom, but she knew something wasn't right. There should have been something inside it. She wrapped it in a tissue and pushed it deep down into the kitchen garbage. She desperately scrubbed her hands, trying to get rid of the filth that stained her body.

The baby, now sensing Debbie's fear, had started crying. When Debbie returned to Christopher, he was gone. The rest of the night was lived out in fear – a fear that would forever be associated with those walls. But when she returned home for the evening, Debbie by all accounts presented as though nothing had happened. She looked normal. This was the first time she had learned to hide within herself.

Her first inclination was to tell her mom, but what good would it do now? Days before, Angie had suffered from a nearly fatal gunshot wound. That, coupled with her mother's failing health, seemed like too much to burden her with.

Besides, what if this really was her fault? She could have fought more – kicked him harder, maybe bit him. Debbie wrestled endlessly with these thoughts. Her conclusion – maybe she actually wanted this to happen. Maybe in some twisted way, she had asked for this. Maybe she had given him signals, flirted too much. The embarrassment it would cause her family was too much. So Debbie kept quiet. She endured silently as the abuse got worse.

School, her once sacred and safe place, became corridors of chaos, hallways of horror. In between classes, Juan would find her and force her into dark corners. She tried to wear the tightest pants possible, but he still managed to force his hands into her pants, into her. When he had finished with her, Debbie would make her way to the bathroom and eliminate her blood-soaked panties. He literally ripped her apart. She would bleed for days after he attacked her.

On one occasion, he forced her into a bathroom and proceeded to rape her. A teacher happened to walk in that day and found the two of them, but rather than reporting the behavior to the principal, she said she was, "Letting them off the hook." Debbie was too young, too estranged from reality to know to tell someone what was happening to her. From him she learned that sex was not the same as affection. He had dragged her down into a world where she had no voice, no feelings, no meaning. She was caught, strangled in his web of destruction and defeat. She did not acknowledge the world around her, including her family. She felt damaged, like no one else would ever want her; and the worst part of it was that each time he violated her, she became more and more attached to him. She was naïve to what a healthy relationship should be, and assumed that this was her expected role – to succumb to his sexual desires at all times. The more she was raped, the more she thought she loved him.

Eventually, Juan would move to another state. Though the abuse physically stopped at that time, the hole it left in her spirit remained forever. This traumatic life event could potentially be the first domino in a series of unfortunate, unhealthy sexual experiences for Debbie.

One of the most common psychological consequences of rape is self-blame. Victims blame themselves for what has happened to them. *I shouldn't have worn that dress. I shouldn't have made him wait so long. I must have wanted it.* Other common emotional and psychological effects of rape include post-traumatic stress disorder (PTSD), depression, flashbacks, borderline personality disorder, sleep disorders, eating disorders, dissociative identity disorder, guilt, distrust of others, anger, feelings of personal powerlessness, and many more. Debbie suffered a number of these psychological reactions.

Throw the word "puberty" into any given rough life situation and the whole thing seems to exponentially become more chaotic. Juan leaving threw Debbie into a deep sadness and emptiness. Debbie began experimenting with cigarettes about this time. Smoking became a stress reliever. She often seemed irritated for no reason. Her dynamic personality grew more extreme – very high or very low. Her mother nicknamed her the little girl with the curl after a nursery rhyme by Henry Wadsworth Longfellow.

There was a little girl,
Who had a little curl,
Right in the middle of her forehead.
When she was good,
She was very good indeed,
But when she was bad she was horrid.

She would at time dress above her age, claiming to be "almost an adult," and then would want to play with her Barbie dolls, but only in secret because she believed she was too old to want to play with dolls. So many dualities began to surface in her teenage years.

Debbie was unsure of who she was and who she was yet meant to be. Her feelings were likely expounded due to the hormonal changes occurring in her pubescent frame. Debbie hated seeing her body change. Who Debbie felt she was, and who she saw in the mirror never matched. She felt much younger than she was and seeing her body change before her eyes was troubling. She thought maybe this she could control. Maybe if she looked like a child, she would be left alone.

Debbie developed anorexia. She was extremely picky about her eating and became very thin. She was a beautiful girl starting to develop breasts and fill out with curves. She couldn't stand it. By many standards she was sexually enticing. But Debbie didn't feel that way. She didn't really have sexual thoughts as a teenager. Because of her rape, Debbie associated sex with filth. But sex in a relationship was all Debbie knew. She had no positive relationship experiences to relate to.

Her parents weren't healthy role models in this respect. Larry never showed any emotion, much less any sexual inclinations towards his wife in Debbie's presence, and Joyce was always insecure about her sexuality. Larry would tease her about her body, saying she was too soft, "gaining a little weight there," so Joyce tended to be more reserved. She always seemed shocked if a man paid her any attention or thought she was beautiful.

People forever thought Debbie was beautiful. You would be a fool not to think so. But her beauty came with insecurities that left her wide open to be taken advantage of. Many men in her teenage life scared or humiliated her. One man had her use newspaper as blankets, and would smell her private area to make sure she wasn't cheating. Though she was fearful during her first sexual experience, she became numb to the fear of sex. As she became more and more sexually experienced, in its place grew fear of loneliness. She sacrificed her own feelings and needs to prevent the feeling of abandonment.

In her world, sex was the ticket to keeping a man around. After Juan, Debbie started dating again around age 16, and she would continue to have sexual relations with each one. Teenage guys only want one thing, and if she gave it up, they'd usually come back for more. Right after sex, each guy would seem very attentive, pleased with her. Debbie craved this approval.

Debbie entered East Bay High School as a member of the 1994 freshman class. Her future husband, Owen LaFave, also attended East Bay, though the two were not friendly until later. She joined the chorus and was on the homecoming court. She even began casually dating the senior football star.

That is, until her brief period as a lesbian. Following the betrayal of her breakup with Nick and the horrific rapes she endured by Juan, Debbie began acting erratically and very much unlike herself. Her beauty caught the attention of nearly everyone in school – boys and girls. One female student in particular took an extra special look at Debbie. For now, let's call her, Katie. Katie was two years older than Debbie and for about two months she captivated Debbie. Debbie morphed from a rising pop star to a rocker chick that listened to bands whose lead singers were outspoken lesbians. In conversations with her mother, Debbie would often point out people who were gay. But if this were merely an experimental phase,

Debbie committed to the experiment. The girls often met at Katie's house and fooled around together. They kissed and were sexual with each other. Katie introduced Debbie to marijuana and the two occasionally got high together before engaging in sexual acts. But their rebellious romance was short lived.

Debbie and Katie were seen openly kissing at school. Rumors soon spread around campus that the beautiful, intelligent, wholly desired Debra Beasley was "doing it" with a girl. The principal who had gotten wind of the rumors flying made a school wide announcement that kissing on school property, especially same-sex kissing, was strictly prohibited. There was no doubt in anyone's mind that this decree was aimed directly at Katie and Debbie. Eventually, Debbie's chorus teacher reached out to her mother and expressed concerns about Debbie's unusual behavior.

"It just isn't like her," she confided to Mrs. Beasley.

Within a few months, Debbie would attempt suicide twice. She first attempted to take a bottle of Tylenol; second Debbie took a razor to her wrists. Both times called for trips to the hospital. Her mother was in shock and didn't know what to do. She decided to seek out professional help. Debbie began seeing an outside counselor, Dr. Roach, on a weekly basis. Dr. Roach seemed most concerned about Debbie's anorexia and less concerned about her bout of lesbianism. He believed she would be in a new relationship in no time. He did recommend, however, that Debbie change schools in hopes of her being able to start fresh. He wrote a letter recommending the change in placement and Joyce arranged for Debbie to be pulled from East Bay and enrolled at Bloomingdale High School. She thought she was doing what was best for her daughter, moving her away from a potentially shameful and damaging environment. Debbie had always been attracted to people who were controlling or manipulative, and the Beasleys felt that maybe she had been manipulated by this girl.

Debbie joined the chorus at Bloomingdale and made the elite group. After boys, singing was Debbie's greatest love. She felt most alive when the spotlight hit her on stage. This was her biggest focus. Debbie, once a straight-A student, didn't care so much about her academics anymore. Community college was the expectation she had for herself. She made friends almost instantly, and also formed a new relationship with an older man, Kevin. At this time, Debbie's sister Angie was engaged to Kyle O'Dell. The two families often spent time together and Debbie was introduced to Kyle's older brother Kevin.

Kevin was the first long-term boyfriend Debbie had. Debbie was drawn to him because he seemed to want to take care of her – almost as a father would. His affection replaced that which her father Larry often withheld. He would buy her things and take her places. She fell in love with him quickly. He was different in that he was not just a lover – he was her first love. The two dated from Debbie's sophomore year in high school to part way through her senior year. Debbie would often skip school to be with Kevin. Kevin's sex drive was relatively low, and Debbie felt relieved of her duties.

Debbie felt like this man could be her prince charming, but in reality, he was more like a toad – or a typical southern redneck. Later, Debbie learned that he had a severe alcohol addiction, which, among other things, prevented him from keeping an erection. After a few beers Kevin would turn nasty. Her prince charming morphed into a verbally abusive, obnoxious boar of a man. He would treat her heinously, but Debbie crumbled against his harsh voice. Only her sister Angie ever stood up to Kevin in the face of how he treated her younger sister. Angie wasn't afraid of anything or anyone, and she certainly wasn't going to let this loser treat her baby sister this way – even if this loser was her soon to be brother-in-law. For two years, Debbie and Kevin tried to make it work. Her world shattered again when they broke up. He became more violent with her, but despite her fear, she longed to be with him. She was attached. The two ultimately split as a result of his addictions, but since Angie married Kevin's brother, the two remained in contact.

In December of 1997, Joyce Beasley had recently been diagnosed with breast cancer and was battling with her own health. After several rounds of chemotherapy, Joyce elected to have a double mastectomy. She was on bed rest for 6 weeks following the procedure. For the first time in her life, Debbie distanced herself from her mother. She could not be near her, and any time she was, she often asked her mother if she was going to die. Her mother's reassurances did little to calm her anxiety. She would often tell her mother that if she (Joyce) died, that Debbie would surely have to kill herself because she could not bear to live without her mother. As much as she depended on her mother, she could not be around sickness. She could not stand to see the one person on whom she relied the most, in a position that made her weak. Joyce needed to be cared for. Friends of the family often scolded Debbie for not being there for her mother, but Debbie didn't know how to care for someone else. She only knew that she needed her mother to care for her.

After Kevin, Debbie began dating Andrew with whom she had remained friends since elementary school. She finished out her high school career at Bloomingdale High whilst coupled with Andrew. Andrew was active in his local church and Debbie began to attend functions with him more regularly. She enjoyed being in a body of spiritual believers. It brought sweet memories from childhood to her mind. But though she ought to have felt more stable, Debbie continue to be plagued with bouts of depression and periods of ceaseless crying for no apparent reason. Andrew had a jealous side to him and could never quite get over the fact that Debbie had dated Kevin and still spent time with her former love. This was their most frequent argument. Occasionally she would become so frustrated with Andrew that she was thrown into a fit of rage and would yell and hit him. Andrew told her that she needed professional help and so Debbie saw a psychiatrist who prescribed her Zoloft for depression. Debbie continued to take the medication, but felt little difference.

On one occasion, Debbie was waiting for Andrew at Angie's house. While waiting for his arrival, she and Kevin went out for drinks. When they returned, Andrew was waiting for them. Smoke seemed to come out of his ears. He insisted that Debbie was cheating on him with Kevin despite her denials. Andrew's anger and jealousy overtook him and he swung a punch at Kevin's face. Kevin retaliated and the two wailed on each other, but Andrew was letting out months of built up angst and aggression on the other. Kevin, fumbling from the buzz of his beers a few minutes earlier, was taking a stern beating. Debbie yelled, pleaded for the two of them to stop. Tears streamed down from her blue eyes as Angie, once again Debbie's hero, slammed open the door and got right in between the flying fists. The two were separated and this time it was Angie who struck the blows. She got in several good punches on Andrew before the flashing blue lights of a police car signaled the end of the gangs night.

However, Andrew was not satisfied. A few weeks later, when he knew the Beasleys and their daughter would be out of the house, he broke in and headed towards Debbie's room. He broke into her diary in search of anything that might spark the fire to his burning jealousy. When Joyce and Larry discovered what had happened, it was made clear that he was no longer welcome in their home. And yet despite all of this, Debbie continued to date him. Like a hamster on a wheel, she kept spinning and spinning in relationships that were taking her nowhere.

UNIVERSITY OF SOUTH FLORIDA

Debbie had always imagined herself attending a community college after high school, so when she received her acceptance letter from the University of South Florida (USF) she was positively elated. She enrolled in classes for the Fall 1998 semester as a college freshman. USF has four campuses, but the main campus is located in the heart of Tampa, Florida stretching out across a 1,748-acre tract of land. The lush campus is full of huge oak trees and tall palms, and most uniquely with billows and billows of bougainvillea. Nine schools and colleges are located on this campus, including, on the undergraduate level, the colleges of Arts and Sciences, Business Administration, Education, Engineering, Fine Arts and Nursing.

Though Debbie's declared major was English Literature, she knew she wanted to be a teacher. She realized her strong desire to help children while taking Young Adult Literature. She wanted to open up the eyes and minds of children and youth to the world of literature. Never before had she been more inspired or driven towards a goal. But classes were tough, and tuition was expensive. Like many young college students, Debbie worked several jobs to help cover educational expenses and daily spending money. She waitressed at a local restaurant and also worked as a bank teller. It certainly wasn't the "dream job," but everyone has to pay bills some how. Everything seemed to be going her way. She had a nice boyfriend, her mood had somewhat stabilized, and she was doing well in her classes. Never did she think that in a few weeks, her whole world would be rocked.

The Phyllis P. Marshall Center, more so than any other campus facility, serves as a focal point for daily activity for students, faculty, alumni, guests, and visitors. It's basically the local hangout for students between classes. You'll often find students visiting each other, clubs handing out brochures, study groups dutifully preparing for their next test or assignment, and of course, food. Many days Debbie would venture here between classes and sit alone or with Andrew to pass the time.

But one fateful day in February 1999 after a class let out in Cooper Hall, Debbie decided not to make the hike to the Marshall Center, but rather, veered right to the Subway right next to the building. She briskly walked to down the cobblestone sidewalk and swung the door open. It was unusually brisk outside for winter in Florida and she welcomed the heat of the ovens. She was carefully perusing the menu displayed above the sandwich line when she unexpectedly felt a firm tap on her right shoulder followed by an, "Excuse me."

She turned around, assuming it was Andrew or a classmate, but was taken about by a distantly familiar, yet incredibly handsome face.

"Owen!" she exclaimed. She could not believe her eyes. She hadn't seen Owen since her early days at East Bay.

Owen seemed equally as shocked to see Debbie. He asked her what she was doing here and she explained that she had just begun her freshman year. She could not shake the smile off of her face. Owen invited her to eat with him and a friend, so she grabbed her sandwich and sat down. After they ate, she and Owen spent the rest of the afternoon in the sunshine talking about where they had been, what they've each been up to, friends, family, and dreams for the future. Owen talked about the fraternity he had joined and how he had discovered that he really didn't want to be a doctor as he had long thought he was going to become. Instead, he was pursuing a business major. Debbie talked about her literature classes and the idea of becoming an English teacher. She was beautiful and bright, and Owen was very immediately taken with her, and to be quite honest, she was taken with him as well.

In the course of their afternoon conversation, Owen asked Debbie what she had done for Valentine's Day with Andrew. She explained that Andrew didn't particularly care for that kind of "company-created romanticism." Owen looked taken aback.

"Didn't he get you a present?" he asked.

"No, he didn't get me anything," she responded.

"Well, personally I think that's ridiculous. A girl like you deserves way better than that," Owen stated in a cool, off the cuff honesty.

Debbie's stomach fluttered. She asked for Owen's number and pager number, and he asked for hers. Over the next few days, Owen was always at the forefront of Debbie's mind. Even while she was with Andrew she seemed to lag behind him as a result of her daydreaming. They set up a date for the following weekend.

Debbie had never in her life experienced this sort of kind attention from a man. Owen was polite, handsome, and held the door open for her. He treated her like a true gentleman should treat a lady. Debbie broke up with Andrew a few days after her first date with Owen. After that, it was game on.

Just a few weeks into dating him, Debbie had a brilliant idea! She asked Owen to join her on an all expenses paid trip to California. She had been saving all of her extra money for this trip to spend time with her cousin and couldn't think of anyone she would rather have accompany her. As she did with most life decisions, she told her mother about her impending vacation. Joyce tried to dissuade her from her own impulsivity, but Debbie insisted it was a completely logical idea and she intended to follow through.

She was excited to spend several days alone with Owen. The two would be sharing a room and bed together. Debbie could tell that Owen wanted her. It was difficult not to think so when every man she had ever known had used her for her body. But with Owen she wanted things to be different. He was different than any of her former boyfriends and she didn't want to ruin it by rolling in the sack too early.

When they arrived in their hotel room, they dropped their bags and checked out the space they would be sharing. Owen casually laid down on the bed and Debbie cuddled up next to him. He slipped his hand behind her neck and gently pulled her in for a long kiss. Debbie let her hands run up and down his torso, her blood stirring. He was strong and so attractive, but she was nervous. She pulled back and looked into his eyes.

"Owen, do you think we could *not* right now? I just, I don't want to ruin anything," she asked him with eyes downcast. In the brief pause while she awaited his response, she had flashbacks of her past relationships. Then he smiled at her reassuringly. He kissed her gently on the lips and agreed that they should wait – it was too soon. Debbie was relieved, and oddly even more attracted to him.

It was only a few more weeks before the two would both shed their inhibitions and their clothing to share in the most intimate of acts between two people.

One night at Owen's house, Debbie's mother phoned her and told her that her paternal grandmother had passed away. While this wasn't a complete shock to Debbie as she had been diagnosed with cancer, the news came sooner than she expected and it shook her. She hung up the phone with her mom and just sobbed.

She leaned into Owen's chest and he wrapped her in his arms. He kissed the top of her head, then her tears, her lips. She leaned into his kisses. He was a comforting distraction from the pain wreaking havoc on her heart. He gently pulled down the strap of her tank top and she pulled on his shirt. They continued to undress each other until they were completely naked, rubbing their bodies against each other. He was on top of her, breathing heavily. He slipped inside her and immediately Debbie started crying again. It was too soon for this. She had wanted to wait. She felt violated again.

Owen asked her if she was ok, if she wanted him to stop. But it was too late. Now it had already happened.

He was the one she wanted everything to go perfectly with. He was charming, smooth, and always knew what to say. Debbie felt more connected to him than to any other man she had ever known. More than that, she felt safe. Owen protected her and treated her like she was the biggest prize to be won. Owen made her want to be a better person. She quit smoking. She stopped taking her medication. (Owen didn't really believe in medication as an answer to your problems.) He made her want to believe all of the wonderful things he said to her – that she was beautiful, and smart; that she could do anything she wanted to. She was happier than she had been in a long while.

But things were not constantly blissful for the couple. They each had their share of faults too that often came to a heated rise. Both tended to be stubborn and nearly always thought they were right. Owen enjoyed partying and drinking with his fraternity brothers more often than Debbie cared for. There were times when she was happy to go out drinking with the guys, but often she would much rather have just stayed at home. For periods of time, Debbie would avoid friends, not return phone calls, and generally be curt with people. As Owen's expected arm candy, this was unacceptable and caused many an argument.

After Debbie's grandmother passed away she relapsed with her anorexia. She became obsessive over her weight. At first Owen was supportive of her increased desire to hit the gym with him, but eventually he became exceedingly annoyed with Debbie's bizarre eating habits and compulsive checking in the mirror. Debbie's face and body were incredibly thin. This normally 130-pound woman had shrunk down to a mere 107lbs. She was a shadow of her former self. In addition, Debbie began dressing more and more provocatively. As she shrunk, so did her clothing. At first Owen appreciated this sexier side of Debbie, but this soon aggravated him as well. Didn't she know that some things were better left to the imagination? That some things were just meant for him?

On their first dating anniversary, Owen went to Mardi Gras in Louisiana for the weekend. Debbie was extremely jealous about this. Her mind raced with suspicion and anxiety. She *knew* he must have been cheating. Out of spite, without verification, Debbie decided to seek her own form of revenge. If

Owen was going to be out partying and having a great time, she certainly wasn't going to wait around playing the doting naïve girlfriend who sits at home in anticipation of his return. No, she was going to go out too. Debbie slipped into a tiny mini skirt and adjusted her skintight black top, pulling it down to prominently display her newly enhanced breasts. She applied her signature red lipstick, pursed her lips, and with a final tussle of her hair, she approved of herself.

Debbie still lived at home. On her way out, Joyce caught sight of her out of the corner of her eye. She was quite obviously displeased. Debbie rolled her eyes at her mother's concern that she was dressed too "provocatively." What did she know about fashion anyway? She brushed off her mother's concerns with a wave of the hand as she strutted out the door. She was headed to one of the weekly fraternity parties she often went to with Owen. This would be the first she attended solo.

She sauntered through the door and let the beat of the music drive her steps and the swing of her hips. She could feel the eyes in the room turning in her direction. She reveled in the attention. Someone offered her a red solo cup fill with some sort of drink mix, which she readily accepted ready to drink her worries away.

The next morning she woke up to some guy kissing her neck. She felt incredibly dizzy and couldn't for-the-life-of-her remember anything that happened after that initial drink. She peeled this half drunken bozo off of her body and drove herself back home. When she arrived her mother looked concerned and asked her where she had been all night. Debbie confided in the one person whom she always ran to in times of turmoil. She confessed to her mother that she had been at a party and thought she might have been drugged. She was confused and didn't know what to do. Her mom, like always, comforted her – she assured Debbie that she had done nothing wrong and that everything was going to be ok.

Debbie's whole world was her mom. The dependency and closeness she felt towards her was unexplainable. It sometimes hindered her relationships with other people, even those closest to her: Owen, and her sister Angie. At the time, Angie was going through a nasty divorce with her husband. Their mother was spending a lot of time with Angie, helping her pack her belongings and move to a new apartment. The time spent between Joyce and Angie bothered Debbie to no end. She was jealous of the attention her mother was showing towards Angie. Like a child, Debbie would throw temper tantrums about their relationship. She was nasty towards Angie and clung to her mother at any chance she could.

One night the two sisters blew up at each other. It ended with Debbie storming out saying that she didn't need Angie anyway. She distanced herself from Angie and her mother. Neither sister would cave and call the other to make-up because they both vehemently believed the other wronged them. Joyce eventually learned that Angie was pregnant which was a miracle in its own right. For you see, after Angie's shotgun accident a few years earlier, the doctors discovered that some of the bullets had gotten lodged internally and with that much lead running through her body, they concluded that it would be extremely unlikely that she would carry a child to term. Debbie's mother was thrilled at the news and hurriedly shared it with Debbie. Debbie was happy for her sister at first, but as her mother continued to explain that she would need to be spending larger amounts of time with Angie, as her pregnancy was very delicate and high risk at this time, Debbie turned cold. She ran into Owen's arms and threw all of her dependencies onto him, continuing to distance herself from those whom she felt had hurt her so deeply – her mother and sister.

The relationship between Owen and Debbie was cyclical at best. Debbie seemed to go through several personalities in relatively short periods of time. She constantly switched her dependency from Owen to her mother and back again. She needed someone to always have her attention and focus. She needed to know that she was number one in this person's life. Her mother sometimes joked with Owen that she had done the best she could in raising Debbie and now it was his turn. Their relationship was less like a merry-go-round, and more like a roller coaster of breathtaking highs and stomach turning lows. Their physical connection was electric and their emotional connection for each other was undeniable during the steady times, but with Debbie's rapid mood swings and outbursts they two were faces with tremendous hurdles to overcome.

Their frustration came to a blow in January 2001 during the Gasparilla Pirate Festival. For those of you who might not be familiar with this festival, it's basically a giant party in Tampa. Legend has it that a pirate named José Gaspar sailed from his native country in the late 1700s to the sparsely inhabited coast of Southwest Florida and made a secret island base south of Tampa in Charlotte Harbor. For the next two decades, Gaspar is said to have plundered many ships and taken many female hostages as he roamed the coasts of the Gulf of Mexico on his ship, the Florida Blanca. His exploits came to a sudden end in 1821 when, to avoid being captured by the schooner USS Enterprise, he wrapped himself in the ship's anchor chains and threw himself overboard while shouting "Gasparilla dies by his own hand, not the enemy's!"

Despite this colorful history, there is no evidence that a pirate named Gaspar or Gasparilla ever operated off the Florida coast. Nevertheless, since the festival's establishment in 1904, each year nearly 1,000,000 people make their way to Tampa to celebrate the pirates' takeover over the city. A parade of pirate "ship" floats makes its way from the coast to downtown. The "krewe" members throw onlookers beads, coins, and other various trinkets in commemoration of the event.

This particular day was a beautiful one – the kind that people who don't live in Florida dream about. It was sunny with a high of 70°F and nary a cloud in the clear blue sky. Debbie and Owen were amongst the crowd of twenty-somethings ready to spend some fun in the sun. They were with several of Owen's fraternity brothers and their dates. Beers were flowing and everyone was laughing and having a good time. Owen was particularly vivacious in this setting: cracking jokes and making quick-witted conversation with everyone.

At some point during the festivities, he excused himself; said he needed to "drain the snake." He made his was over to a row of porta-potties and got in line. Debbie followed him with her eyes thinking about how disgusting porta-potties were. She couldn't imagine being anywhere near such filth. Just as she was about to turn around to chat with the group, she noticed Owen casually chatting up an attractive girl standing behind him. He made it look so easy, just casually talking over his shoulder at her, throwing her a cheeky smile. Debbie could feel the hairs prick down her neck. Jealousy stirred her heart.

Surely he'll ignore her completely and stop indulging her. No? The jerk is just going to keep on flirting with her in front of me? She's not even that pretty. Doesn't she have anything better to do? Ugh, I bet he thinks she's hot. Whatever!

Owen finished his business and sauntered over, rejoining their group. Debbie couldn't control herself any longer. She laid into him. How dare he talk to another girl right in front of her! He was such a pig. What kind of desperate ass person would talk to a girl like that?

Owen, caught off guard in front of his friends, didn't take any of this laying down. He got right back in her face and said how sick he was of her jealousy, of her anorexia. He said she was a miserable person and that he was through! He stormed away headed to the car and Debbie, immediately regretting her actions, raced to catch him.

Owen drove Debbie back to her house. He remained silent as she pleaded with him to reconsider. She didn't think he would leave. She was devastated. They pulled up into the driveway and Owen turned off the ignition, got out of the car, and slammed the door behind him. Debbie was crying like a baby, screaming his name. Hearing the commotion, Joyce and Larry Beasley opened the front door. Owen stood outside and spoke to Debbie's parents. He said she was crazy and that he was done. He couldn't deal with her anymore. He tried, but he couldn't make it work. She was nuts. Debbie heard his words, but didn't register them. She had dropped to the ground and was grasping his leg like she had done to her mother when she dropped her off at preschool.

She heard her mother start reasoning with Owen. She told him all the reasons why he should reconsider, she urged him to remember the good times. Her father said little, if anything at all. He probably didn't care one way or the other.

Ultimately, Owen did reconsider, but on one condition: Debbie had to resume her psychiatrist visits and explicitly follow any instructions, including taking any medications, that were given to her. This was the first time the two had talked openly about her mental health. She concentrated hard on what he said. He wanted her to get help. He was going to give her a second chance. She hadn't lost him. She wasn't rejected again. Debbie hugged him in a sign of agreement.

Their problems didn't disappear overnight, but for a time, their relationship finally seemed to settle down into a more consistent rhythm.

BUTTERFLIES

As fate would have it, tragedy would befall the Beasley family long before the incidents that made their youngest daughter a household name. After Owen gave her a second chance, Debbie committed herself more than ever to her relationship with him to the continued demise of her familial relationships. Debbie was still estranged from her sister Angie when the Beasley's got the phone call.

On April 18, 2001, Angie was driving in her 1998 Nissan Altima after going out for pizza with friends. She approached a four-way stop intersection, stopped, and proceeded to turn left towards her apartment. Another car approached the intersection, a 1992 Jeep Wrangler, driven by Army Captain Joseph Piotrowski, who had spent the day preparing to return to civilian life. Police records show that Piotrowski had previously violated traffic rules. The previous year he sideswiped another vehicle and drove away from the scene, only to nearly avoid a collision with a police officer about an hour later. He failed a sobriety test and refused a blood-alcohol test, but was not arrested. Maybe the police officers involved were sympathetic to the Army Captain adjusting to his new life, maybe they were feeling particularly generous that night. Either way, Piotrowski left with only a citation for improper lane change and fleeing the scene of an accident.

The day before he was expected to appear in court for charges from the same accident, he was again pulled over for drunk driving, only this time, his license was automatically suspended for 18 months after he *again* refused a blood-alcohol test.

Official police records say that on the night Angie was having pizza with friends, Piotrowski stopped at a liquor store to purchase two half-pint bottles of Jack Daniels, which he drank in his car in the parking lot.

The Beasley's house phone rang at about 10 o'clock that night. It was unusual for the phone to ring so late. Both Joyce and Debbie answered the phone.

A male voice spoke into the phone. "Is this the mother of Angela Beasley?" Debbie quieted, but remained on the line.

"Yes, this is she," replied Joyce. The officer on the line proceeded to tell Mrs. Beasley that a drunk driver had hit her 20-week pregnant daughter's car earlier that evening. Angela Beasley and her unborn daughter, whom she had named Madison, died on impact. Captain Piotrowski had slammed into Angie's car. He was driving with a blood alcohol level three times the legal limit.

Debbie cried out in agony that night. She had not yet made amends with her sister and felt an incredible guilt on top of overwhelming sadness. Unless you have experienced that kind of loss, it is difficult to imagine. Her mother cried and cried. Her father, as always, showed very little emotion. While Joyce and Debbie clung to each other, Larry withdrew deep into himself.

His words that night, however, cut deep into the heart of his youngest daughter: "I have lost my only child."

These traumatizing words rang so loudly in Debbie's soul, she would never forget them. After the night of Angie's death, Debbie too would withdraw deep within herself.

Nearly 500 people attended Angie's visitation and funeral. Nearly all of them showed some type of emotion – except Debbie. She spoke at the funeral, but as she spoke the words, she felt numb. She shed no tears. To everyone else, Debbie must have seemed extremely composed. Truthfully, she had hardened her heart to the pain. She delivered her speech robotically, without pausing for emotion.

The entire night while her mother cried and hugged the guests, Debbie dutifully performed these acts but never displayed any emotion. Her beautiful blue eyes were flat, as if frozen over.

Grief is something everyone experiences, and each person needs to find a way through the healing process after loss. There is no one "right" way to grieve, and there is no way to anticipate exactly how the feelings of sadness, anger, loss, and loneliness will heal and resolve. Some have described the grieving process as a roller coaster, filled with highs and lows. Over time the roller coaster evens out so the highs and lows are more manageable, but the big ups and downs can reappear, especially at important family events, anniversaries, holidays, or other special occasions. People who have suffered grief do say that it will get better with time and the support of friends and loved ones.

Debbie threw herself back into her routine of schoolwork, part-time work, working out, and seeing Owen. Owen was her biggest support system. She confessed to him about the pain that it caused her to know she had not been able to make amends, and the jealous feelings she had towards Angie. She had once thought, "Good, now I don't have to share Mom with her." She would go through periods of being extremely angry with her mother too. Debbie would lash out at her mother, targeting her weakness, as she herself was grieving.

Debbie became obsessed with butterflies. She started noticing them around her after her grandmother's passing and even more so after Angie's. She took the sight of butterflies as a sign that Angie and her grandmother with still around her, supporting her. Despite objections from Owen, Debbie had two butterflies tattooed on her lower back in memory of her sister and grandmother. She also had Angie's name written in Chinese lettering – the symbols for An Ji – place on her lower pelvic area.

Sleeping was difficult. It was increasingly difficult for Debbie to fall asleep at night and when she did, she was plagued with nightmares. She cried out for her mother, calling her, "Mommy!" as she had as a little girl. She seemed to be regressing, debilitating. She wasn't able to make any decisions on her own, but hated when other people made decisions for her. They were never right. She couldn't focus. She would tell stories and stop in the middle, forgetting what she was talking about. When other people would talk to her, she would often interject as if they hadn't been talking and begin with her own conversation. She seemed disconnected from the world around her.

That August, the Army held a Court Martial in Georgia for Captain Piotrowski. Both Debbie and her mother gave key witness testimonies. Joyce told the court about Debbie's difficulty sleeping and about her calling out in the middle of the night. "Debbie is pretty much a basket case," she stated.

"I have been depressed," Debbie stated for the court. "It's hard to concentrate on anything but that," she said. When asked how her sister's death has made her feel these last weeks she said, "Angry. I'd snap at my family for no reason. I've been sick. I've lost a piece of me. She was the person that I looked up to, that I confided in, that I admired. She had a smile that would light up a room. She was, she was - me and mom said that she was a butterfly...I miss calling her for the little things and talking to her about my problems, things that only she would understand probably.""

Captain Piotrowski was deemed guilty to two counts of manslaughter. He was dismissed from the Army and will serve 30 years in prison for the death of Angela Beasley and her unborn daughter.

Owen graduated from college the summer after Angie's death. He accepted a position as in the real-estate credit department of Florida Bank (later to become Mercantile Bank). Debbie was finishing up her last year as a student at USF. Though her degree would be in English, Debbie was interested in teaching and as such, she was required to participate in an internship. She successfully completed her student teaching at Weightman Middle School in Wesley Chapel. By all standards, including the measure with which she was evaluated, Debbie was an excellent educational prospect. She was well prepared for her lessons and conducted herself with the utmost professionalism and respect for herself and her students. Both her university supervisor and the principal of Weightman gave her glowing recommendations and praises.

As graduation approached, Debbie's thoughts turned towards work. She was finally going to be a teacher. She had dreamed of this moment and could hardly believe the time had come to apply for an official teaching position. She originally had wanted to be an English teacher at the high school level, but reconsidered after an advisor at USF cautioned her that a young, attractive teacher surrounded by testosterone driven teens could be particularly disadvantageous. Her certificate of education would make her eligible to teach grades 6-12, so Debbie targeted her search to middle school positions.

After sending dozens of resumes and completing applications, Debbie interviewed at several schools in the area. One in particular however, stood out to her: Greco Middle School. The pros for accepting this position were numerous – located in Temple Terrace, the school was close to home, but not in her regular shopping area (no need to fear running into students while making her Publix runs); she liked the principal; and the student population was challenging. Much of the student population at Greco was considered low in the socio-economic spectrum. Many of these students came from disadvantaged homes, and the word around the block was that the kids were bad at Greco. There was a host of emotional and behavior problems. But unlike many first year teachers, none of this scared Debbie. She saw this as an opportunity to have a greater impact on her students.

The open position was for remedial reading. Debbie had imagined herself opening the minds of her students to the world of fine literature. In this position, Debbie would instead be faced with the difficult task of teaching basic reading skills to struggling students. These students read well below their grade level and were at risk of failing, if not dropping out of school altogether.

Owen was not in favor of this potential work environment. Neither was Debbie's mother. Owen wanted Debbie to pick a different school. Joyce warned Debbie of her concerns, but ultimately told her to follow the path of her own choosing. That

Butterflies

was all that Debbie needed to confirm her decision and she accepted the position at Greco Middle School.

Debbie had been dating Owen for nearly four years around this time. They had both graduated and were eager to pursue the next step in their relationship. Since they were both still living at home, they were itching to get a place of their own. On weekends the couple would spend time looking at potential homes. After searching and budgeting, they excitedly decided on a small townhome in Osprey Run, a new development in Riverview. Debbie's parents helped with the down payment of the $95,000 new construction, and Owen too put down a significant amount. Though they were not even engaged at this point, Debbie was committed to Owen. He was the best boyfriend she had ever had. She was in this for the long hall and couldn't have been more eager to begin a life with him.

As soon as the papers were signed and construction was finished Debbie and Owen moved in together. At first all was well in their new home. They developed a routine of grocery shopping, paying bills, cleaning, and all in all enjoying each other's company. Often times the two would stay at home instead of going out. They were often content wrapping up in each other's arms. Their sex life was at a high. Without the pressures and constraints of having parents around, they were free to embrace as they please. Sometimes that meant multiple times a day.

For the moment everything seemed perfect. But as two people spend more and more time together, their flaws begin to emerge. Owen realized that Debbie was not quite the homemaker he had anticipated. Their quaint little house became more and more disarrayed and dirty. Debbie did do deep cleaning and some cooking, but lacked in organization and domestic styling.

People say that the more time you spend together the more

you're going to get to know the real them. Debbie wasn't intentionally trying to irritate Owen – this was just how she knew how to live. At home her mom did basically everything for her. At times it felt like she just existed in this house with Owen instead of working towards making it their home.

None of this however deterred Owen from his desire to marry the most beautiful woman he had ever known. In February, just a few short months after they purchased their townhouse, Owen whisked Debbie off to New Orleans to propose. Of course, Debbie didn't know that at the time. He had cleverly disguised the trip as a business venture. He even brought loan paperwork to look through on the plane. Debbie had been slightly suspicious up until that point, but after seeing that he had actually brought work with him, she assumed that this was in fact just another business trip.

Debbie was a little disappointed because she thought this would be the time to get engaged. Her mood soured slightly. After they arrived safely in New Orleans, they went to their hotel to check-in. Their room was not quite ready yet but the concierge told them that they could check their things then. To kill some time they walked around the French quarter of New Orleans. They walked around and looked at the buildings, stopping for a light lunch and coffee.

Late in the afternoon Owen guided Debbie to Jackson Square. Owen spotted a horse drawn carriage available for rent. The sign displayed next to the carriage said $40 for half an hour ride. Debbie's nose turned up. She said, "Owen that's too expensive." Owen insisted. "It's romantic and I love you. When will we ever get a chance to do this again?"

Debbie finally gave in. The two climbed into the carriage and Owen spread the blanket across their laps. The clip clop of the horses' hooves on the cobblestone streets was oddly soothing. Debbie felt safe and content sitting there with Owen. She had to admit that this was really special. The carriage pulled up to an old garden in the French Quarter, full of flowers and an iron fence. Debbie watched as the butterflies flitted from flower to flower. Beside her, she felt Owen stir.

By the time she looked over at him, he was down on one knee holding a beautiful ring box, inside of which held the most beautiful ring she had ever seen. She was stunned as she heard him say, "Debbie, I love you very much, you make me extremely happy. I don't want to go on living without you. Will you marry me?" Debbie's eyes well with tears and her throat tightened. She was overwhelmed with love for this man, and she tried to soak in this perfect moment. Owen slipped the ring on her finger and she stared. He looked into her eyes and said, "Well?"

"Yes," she answered. "Of course."

When the couple returned to Florida, word spread about their engagement. Debbie was flooded with words of encouragement and congratulations at home and at school. Her coworkers, some of which had become her dearest friends, we're thrilled by the news. Joyce and Larry threw an engagement party for the couple, with 70 family members and friends in attendance. It was a bit more extravagant than Debbie had anticipated, but the gesture was appreciated. A few of their friends had also recently gotten married. Debbie and Owen were introduced to a wedding planner to help them hone in the details of their own wedding.

Every little girl dreams about her wedding day, And usually they have all the details already picked out except for the groom – and even then sometimes that's fantasize to be the hottest actor or musician at the time. Oddly enough, Debbie was more apathetic in her wedding planning. She often seemed disinterested in making decisions, leaving Owen to dream up their wedding. She did have a few things that she knew she wanted to be included. There were few elements that Debbie took firm stances on – one of which were the colors. Debbie desired a classic contemporary wedding in which the dominant colors were white and black. She also wanted the bridesmaids to carry bouquets of orchids with a butterfly to represent Angie's spirit.

Wedding planning is stressful. There is no way around it. Ideally this would be the beginning of two families merging into one. Owen and Debbie's mom argued about several wedding details, in particular the guest list. Owen had created a guest list and when Joyce tried to add one or two more people to it, Owen would become extremely frustrated.

Joyce said, "If I'm paying for this wedding, I can invite anyone I want to."

Debbie supported her soon-to-be husband's decisions fully. She thought her mom was acting cold. She had been acting this way since Angie's death.

In May 2003, the second trial was held for the drunk driver responsible for the death of Debbie's sister Angela. This time the trial would be held in a Florida criminal court with charges brought on by the State Attorney's office in Tampa. More than a year and a half had passed since the captain's court-martial hearing in Georgia. Despite efforts by his attorney to waive his retrial in Tampa, Capt. Piotrowski faced charges for the death of Angie and her unborn daughter. Normally there is not a retrial by the state after a court-martial, but military prisoners are eligible for parole after serving only a third of their sentence.

BUTTERFLIES

Capt. Piotrowski was due to be released in another three years. The idea of this man being released sickened the Beasley family.

With each trial, it was like an old wound in Debbie's heart reopening. The story was constantly in the media. It was very dramatic for Debbie to watch and relive the night of her sisters passing over and over. She endured questioning and curiosity from strangers 24 hours a day. News channels and reporters constantly contacted Debbie and her family for interviews to tell their story. Debbie's guilt continued to overwhelm her.

Ultimately, Capt. Piotrowski was deemed guilty of two counts of manslaughter and would serve two consecutive sentences of 15 years each. Finally, justice was served, and the Beasley family could go back to their regular lives for a brief time before again rising to the forefront of the media's attention.

It was difficult for Debbie to get overly excited by everything because it overwhelmed her. Even the night before the wedding, it felt to her like just another day. It wasn't until she put on her dress that she really started beaming. And rightly so – she had spent the last several months intensely preparing her body for this moment. Debbie had been religiously tanning and strictly limiting her food intake to fit into this size-6 dress. (For those of you who don't know, this is like a real-life size 2…) She looked as radiant as ever in her crisp white, cap-sleeve gown.

On July 19, 2003 at a church ceremony near Tampa Bay, Owen and Debbie were married. Both Debbie and her bridesmaids held beautiful orchid bouquets with black satin sashes holding the delicate flowers together. Her dream was realized and each woman also carried a butterfly in memory of her dear sister, Angie. After the simple, tender ceremony, these butterflies were released into the warm summer air and Debbie felt an inner peace – her sister was there with her on this special day.

The newly wed couple was blissfully happy. They exchanged heart felt words to each other during the reception – words which now are a distant memory – and it was clear to all that they had eyes only for each other.

Unfortunately though, this happiness, though honest and true, was fleeting and soon their rose colored world would be turned dark and tumultuous.

Photo Gallery

Photo Gallery

Photo Gallery

Photo Gallery

BECOMING A SEXUAL OFFENDER

Research shows that women who are diagnosed with a mental illness are nearly 40% more likely to be victims of sexual assault. But what about the other way around? Are victims of sexual abuse more likely to then become offenders? Most research on this question focuses on boys. Do young boys who are victims of sexual abuse go on to become sexual offenders? Much research shows that this is not causal. However, there seems to be a stigma of this vicious cycle of the abused becoming the abuser. It's probably because in some cases that's what we find.

According to police profiles of child sexual offenders and predators, these people most often offend against children whom they know and with whom they have established a relationship. Nearly 90% of child victims know their offender, with almost half of the offenders being a family member. Of sexual assaults against people age 12 and up, approximately 80 percent of the victims know the offender.

In the majority of cases, abusers gain access to their victims through deception and enticement, seldom using force. Abuse typically occurs within a long-term, ongoing relationship between the offender and victim and escalates over time. While there is a small subset of child sexual abusers who are exclusively attracted to children, the majority of the individuals who sexually abuse children are (or have previously been) attracted to adults. Pressure to be liked and not be talked about negatively by a peer will sometimes cause adolescents or children to avoid fighting back or actively resist. Because of the age difference, children are unable to legally consent to sexual acts. They are often made to feel like willing participants, which further contributes to their shame and guilt.

In a National Public Radio interview from 2011, a former FBI profilist described grooming – a term often used in conjunction with child sex offenders. She said that offenders groom not only the victim (the child), but also parents, colleagues, and the community. It takes several steps to basically seduce a whole variety of people to achieve his goals.

I recently participated in a sexual harassment and abuse awareness training in which the speaker consistently referred to predators using male pronouns. She did make a point however, to clarify that though there is much more data on male predators, females may also be predators. The slide then displayed portraits of well-known female predators. I was stunned to see Debbie's picture among the women. It amazes me that even still, Debbie – a woman I have come to know and respect – could be considered a predator. This just goes to show how iconic her case was and how the affects continue to influence the world today.

Prior to June 2004, Debbie had never been in trouble with the law. She had never been arrested for any other crime and never served any sort of jail time or institutional time. It's hard for her to say exactly what she was thinking. Her thoughts always raced. She began talking freely with her students as if they were peers. She wanted to be like them, so much that she started to listen to their kind of music and dressed in their kind of clothing. She began talking inappropriately with all of her students, talking about sex and using profanity. As the school year came to a close, Debbie pulled further away from Owen and her family, and fell deeper into the lifestyle and mentality of a teenage girl.

Debbie started attending athletic events at Greco. She noticed a basketball player (referred to throughout the remainder of the text as Jack Carpenter) who liked to flirt with her. She liked the attention; she was flattered; so she flirted back. She didn't even think about the fact that he was a kid. She developed a crush on him, shamelessly flirted during the day, and then every night came home to her husband – though Owen was rarely home when she arrived. Often she would be alone on the couch with popcorn and the television for comfort. Debbie saw no wrong in her actions. After all, this boy was nowhere near in the league of her husband. She was very childlike in her behavior, and began to revert back to her teenage relationship experiences. She felt like she had to please the person she was with, and in this case it was a 14-year-old boy. Abuse had left a huge wound gaping in her soul. She used men and other false bandages to heal it. The bandage started to unravel when he came into her life.

He did not arouse her sexually, but she definitely sexually aroused him. She took advantage of that. Debbie knew how to work her body, and make a man want her. Being 14, it wasn't very hard for Jack to fall into the trap this beautiful older woman, his teacher, was laying for him. With hormones raging, it's very easy for young boys to get turned on for almost any reason.

Their relationship was very much that of junior high. She didn't play an adult role. If anything, he did. Believe it or not, he often intimidated her. He was cocky and sometimes aggressive bringing out memories of her past. She began to relive the emotions she felt when she was young. Oddly, she began to feel young again. She giggled often and lost perception of her present reality.

The last day of school was a humid scorcher, as most Florida days are in May. She walked her students to the buses, and waved to them as they left. Student and teachers alike were all looking forward to the long-awaited summer vacation. All that was left to do was finish up some emails, check her messages, and shut down her classroom. She walked the concrete path to the back of the school where her portable was to get her things and noticed that Jack had followed. The pair entered the portable and she shut the door behind them. Jack casually sunk into one of the couches Debbie had set up along the wall and watched her as she moved around the room. They spoke casually and she giggled at his jokes. She asked him what his plans were for the summer – basketball and hanging out.

Debbie was bent over facing away from him putting things in her bag when she felt him behind her. It startled her because she hadn't realized that he had gotten off the couch. He gripped her waist in his strong, large hands and she lost her breath. He kissed her and she him. Her arms folded behind his head. But then Jack attempted to slide his fingers up her shirt and persuade her to take it off. She was very hesitant. As she repeatedly told him no, he became more and more aggressive. So aggressive that he was able to pull her shirt so high up that her bare breasts were exposed. Her mind shattered. Memories of her past flashed before her. How could this have happened to her again? She was not going to let this happen. She would not be controlled, taken advantage of, or manipulated ever again. She would take care of her past once and for all.

In early June, Debbie's mother began to notice that Debbie seemed to be distancing herself from Owen and the family. She and Owen argued more often. They argued about everything from money, to Debbie's laziness in keeping a clean household, to how she dressed, to their sex life, to the idea of starting a family. Right after they were married Debbie talked about wanting to have kids immediately. This was a point of contention because Owen didn't even know if he really wanted to have kids at all. In any way, he absolutely didn't want to have kids right away. He was working hard and was on his way towards a promotion at work. With the promotion came a large pay raise, and Debbie definitely spent money. Mostly on supplies for her classroom, but Owen scrutinized all of her purchases. Especially clothing purchases. He would often question her clothing choices for work, stating that they were not appropriate at all for a teacher of young boys, to which Debbie responded, "They're teenage boys. They don't care what I look like." Tension continued to build within their marriage. It wasn't always like this though. There were good times as well, but it was largely dictated by Debbie's mood. She continued to have cyclical depressive and then overly positive periods.

Owen reached out to Debbie's parents toward the end of May 2004. In an effort to talk with her daughter about any marital troubles that the newlyweds might be experiencing, Joyce suggested the family take their annual beach trip. Debbie's parents, Owen, and she stayed at a beach house for a week every year. This trip, Debbie brought along a new CD she had recently purchased, and wanted to share it with her mom. It was a hip-hop CD that she said, "everybody is listening to." Joyce was appalled. The music was offensive and vulgar. She could not believe that her successful, married daughter was listening to this sort of music. Debbie also spoke about different job opportunities. She wondered about how much money a woman could make as a valet wearing Hooters like shorts. The topics in which she was engaging were very odd – even to those closest to her. Her mother was concerned and confronted her about these concerns. Debbie just laughed it off as she always did, but when pressed became angry and defensive. She didn't think there was anything wrong with the way she was acting, or how she was dressing. No one was going to tell her what she could or couldn't do.

Phone calls from students (mostly from Jack) came in at odd hours throughout the vacation. Debbie would talk with them on her phone late at night, giggling at their stories and sharing details of her life. Joyce and Larry confronted Debbie about these phone calls and warned her of how inappropriate they were. But Debbie didn't care. It was fun. These were her friends. It didn't matter that she was married to a successful man who took care of her, that she had a great job that made her feel alive, and that she had a beautiful house that she made her home. She lost interest in the desire to have a child and start a family. It didn't matter that her life was her dream come true. She was bored. She had become bored with her own life and was supplementing through her students.

Jack and Debbie continued their relationship into summer. While Owen was working, Debbie would drive Jack to play basketball and watch him play. She would lie to her family and give them excuses for why she would leave the house to go and sneak off with Jack. Eventually, Owen and Debbie's parents began to suspect she was having an affair, though they never expected it to be with a 14 year old.

Debbie had sexual intercourse, including oral sex, with Jack on four different occasions. The first time Debbie and Jack had sex, Debbie wanted to back out. He mocked her by calling her a little virgin. She didn't see him as a child, but as a peer. She felt like he was her boyfriend, and he treated her as he would have treated any other girl. The more he wrongly treated her, the more she felt dependent of him. The more he rejected her, or pushed her away, the more obsessed she became. She felt like she would burst if she didn't talk to him on a daily basis. She would get jealous if she saw him talking to another girl. Looking back, she realizes how childlike she was acting. This immaturity is obvious in the recorded phone calls prior to her arrest.

In June 2004, Jack and Debbie went to see his cousin in Ocala. Unbeknownst to Debbie or the boys, Jack's aunt spotted Jack's cousin leaning against Debbie's silver SUV. She called him and questioned what he was doing. He reported that he, Jack, and a friend were shopping for Father's Day presents. Feeling suspicious, she then phoned Jack's mother and asked if she knew that Jack was currently in Ocala. Upon his return home, under intense questioning from his mother, Jack admitted that it was Debbie who had driven them to Ocala and that the two had been intimate that day and on a few other occasions. Mrs. Carpenter immediately contacted the local police office and she and her son gave statements to Officer Thorton.

Jack was able to correctly identify intimate, incriminating details about Debbie's person, personal life, and home. He identified her "Chinese or Japanese" writing tattoo on the small, center of her lower back, two butterfly tattoos on one side of her lower back, and described her three belly-button rings. However, many Greco students had seen her bare midriff. His description of her pubic area was incredibly accurate. It should be noted too, that Jack and his cousin disclosed that they and their friends thought that having sex with Mrs. LaFave was "cool" and that Jack often bragged about it.

Realizing that Jack's clothing may have DNA evidence on it, Officer Thorton transferred the case to the Special Victims Unit. Detective Mike Pridemore assumed the lead role in the investigation. It was through his coaching and strategy that the Temple Terrace police were able to record conversations between Jack and Debbie, which would ultimately lead to her arrest.

Recorded Conversation #1
June 18th 8:30am

Debbie: Hello.

Jack: Hey.

Debbie: Hey. What's up?

Jack: Nothing. What're you doing?

Debbie: Nothing, just drinking coffee and watching TV.

Jack: Oh, really?

Debbie: Yeah. What's up?

Jack: I got up early to talk to you.

Debbie: Oh. Are you okay?

Jack: Yeah. I… me and my mom kind of had an argument last night, but it's fine now.

Debbie: Yeah?

Jack: Uh-huh.

Debbie: I talked to her.

Jack: Oh, you did?

Debbie: Yeah. I called her when I got home last night.

Jack: Oh. How did that go?

Debbie: It was… I mean I just told her, I was like, you know, I'm sorry, bad judgment and I should double check with you, blah, blah, blah.

Jack: Uh-huh. Well, I guess I don't think we should be going to Ocala anymore.

Debbie: No, no.

Jack: But everything went smooth in the portable.

Debbie: Yeah.

Jack: So, whatever. If we decide to do anything again, then that should probably be our place for now.

Debbie: That's true. Are you okay?

Jack: Yeah. I'm fine now.

Debbie: Yeah.

Jack: Uh-huh.

Debbie: I… did you call me last night?

Jack: Yeah.

Debbie: I can't remember if I can get or if… When are you leaving today?

Jack: I don't know yet. I have to talk to my dad.

Debbie: I'm not sure if I'm going to Denver anymore.

Jack: Oh.

Debbie: So maybe when…

Jack: Yeah.

Debbie: Holy Lord, right?

Jack: Yeah, I know. It's kind of crazy, but I'm pretty sure everything is fine now.

Debbie: Good. I totally got… well I told Owen and everything.

Jack: About what?

Debbie: Like, oh no, no, no, no, no – chill. I just said that – I pretty much just told him the whole story.

Jack: Cool.

Debbie: Except, you know, why we went to Ocala.

Jack: Of course.

Debbie: He actually gave me advice on what to say to your mom.

Jack: Yeah?

Debbie: Yeah. Yeah, so…

Jack: All right. Well, you enjoyed yourself yesterday, right?

Debbie: I did. Did you?

Jack: yeah.

Debbie: So it's not *over,* over?

Jack: Nope, not yet.

Debbie: God, Jack– why couldn't you have just said, "No, not yet?"

Jack: I'm sorry.

Debbie: That kind of sucked. Oh, Lord, what am I going to do with you?

Jack: Sorry.

Debbie: Did you end up playing last night?

Jack: Yeah.

Debbie: Was it difficult to play?

Jack: A little. I did pretty good though.

Debbie: Did you?

Jack: Uh-huh.

Debbie: All right, my dear.

Jack: Okay. So you don't have any plans for today?

Debbie: No… I'm just chillin' today. Hello? Are you there? Hello?

Jack: Hello?

Debbie: Hey.

Jack: So after my dad's, after I get back from my dad's, do you want to get together again?

Debbie: Yes, I do.

Jack: Okay.

Debbie: Okay?

Jack: All right.

Debbie: Did you miss me last night?

Jack: Yeah. What can we do this time, do you think?

Debbie: We'll definitely figure out something very local.

Jack: Okay.

Debbie: I will have it all planned out.

Jack: Okay.

Debbie: I hope you have a good weekend.

Jack: You, too.

Debbie: Okay.

Jack: All right. Well, I guess I'll talk to you later.

Debbie: Okay, honey.

Jack: All right.

Debbie: Bye.

Jack: Bye.

Recorded Conversation #2
June 18th

Jack: My dad canceled for the weekend, but my mom says I'm grounded, so I can't do anything.

Debbie: Really?

Jack: Yeah.

Debbie: Your dad canceled?

Jack: Uh –huh.

Debbie: That's kind of shitty.

Jack: Yeah, I know.

Debbie: That sucks.

Jack: I know. I'm going to see him, though. Sometime.

Debbie: Oh, that's good.

Jack: I'm a little worried though.

Debbie: Why?

Jack: Like I don't want you to, like, get pregnant or anything. I was just thinking about it and I was thinking if next time, now that we've had sex about three times, if I should use like a condom or something.

Debbie: Oh, you're being weird.

Jack: Why?

Debbie: Why are you being weird?

Jack: It's just been, I've been thinking about it because I haven't used… I'm just scared. I don't know.

Debbie: Oh – that should be the least of your worries.

Jack: Okay. All right. So are you probably going to Denver or no, you said?

Debbie: No, I'm not going to go.

Jack: Oh, you're not?

Debra: Huh-uh.

Conversation #3
June 18th (A few minutes later)

Jack: Yeah. I was just thinking about it. It's just been like on my mind a lot lately.

Debbie: Yeah? Are you freaking out?

Jack: Yeah: No. I was just… I was just thinking about it and I thought I'd ask you to see how you are feeling about it.

Debbie: Yeah?

Jack: Uh-huh.

Conversation #4 – June 19th 11:18am

Debbie: Hello?

Jack: Hey.

Debbie: Can you hear me?

Jack: Yeah.

Debbie: There's like 20 kids here, screaming.

Jack: Where are you at?

Debbie: I'm at some YMCA…

Jack: Really?

Debbie: … In downtown Tampa.

Jack: Oh.

Debbie: There's like 1,000 kids here.

Jack: Oh.

Debbie: So what's up?

Jack: Nothing much. What are you doing?

Debbie: Nothing. I'm actually holding… Pam has a newborn baby, so I'm kind of holding her right now.

Jack: Oh, really?

Debbie: Yeah, watching all the… My ovaries are hurting listening to all these friggin' kids screaming.

Jack: (laughs)

Debbie: You couldn't pay me enough money to have a kid

right now.

Jack: So do you have any plans for Monday?

Debbie: No, I don't think so.

Jack: Do you want to try to do something Monday?

Debbie: Yeah, that's cool.

Jack: All right, because I'm grounded for the rest of the weekend. You could probably pick me up at the rec.

Debbie: Okay. So how… how… how did everything end up? Is everything okay right now?

Jack: Uh-huh.

Debbie: Yeah?

Jack: All right. Probably you could probably just pick me up here. Is that alright? That would probably be better.

Debbie: Why?

Jack: I don't know. Because I don't know if I'll be able to get a ride to rec. Because my mom is going to be working.

Debbie: Okay.

Jack: All right.

Debbie: So, everything is cool?

Jack: Yeah.

Debbie: Yeah?

Jack: Uh-huh.

Debbie: Sure?

Jack: Yeah. All right, and everything is good with you?

Debbie: Yeah, so far so good.

Jack: All right.

Debbie: Yeah.

Jack: All right. Well…

Debbie: I was a little worried yesterday, but…

Jack: All right. Well about what time do you think you're going to want to pick me up on Monday?

Debbie: I have no idea. I'll call you.

Jack: All right because I don't know if I'm going to be able to talk to you because I'm going to be with my dad tomorrow.

Debbie: Okay. All right.

Jack: All right.

Debbie: Okay. Well, I'll just… I'll talk to you later.

Jack: Okay, then.

Debbie: Okay, bye.

Conversation #5
June 21st ~9:00am

Debbie: Hello?

Jack: Hey.

Debbie: Hey. What are you doing?

Jack: Nothing. What are you doing?

Debbie: Driving.

Jack: Oh, you are?

Debbie: I had to take Owen to work today.

Jack: Huh?

Debbie: I had to take Owen to work today.

Jack: Oh, really? What's wrong with the car that you guys had an accident in?

Debbie: Oh, we totaled it.

Jack: Oh, you did?

Debbie: Yes. It's his car. It's totaled, yeah.

Jack: Oh, All right. So what time are you planning on heading over?

Debbie: Are you sure? Like, I just feel... I mean, I don't want you lying to your mom. I mean, it's like...

Jack: No, it's alright. She's gone in a sales meeting, like all day.

Debbie: Yeah?

Jack: Yeah, I'm positive.

Debbie: I mean, I just... I know you wouldn't, you know, do it unless you were sure.

Jack: I am.

Debbie: I mean, we were just so close last time, you know?

Jack: Yeah.

Debbie: Are you sure, sure?

Jack: Yes.

Debbie: You wouldn't lie to me, would you?

Jack: No.

Debbie: No what?

Jack: Why are you saying that?

Debbie: I don't know. I'm just scared. It was a little freaky last time.

Jack: Oh.

Debbie: And you were just like really dead set on, you know, taking a break.

Jack: Well, I just want to... I just wanted to see you. I thought you wanted to see me, too.

Debbie: No, no, no, no, no, no. Don't take it the wrong way. It's just, you know, I'm looking out.

Jack: Yeah, but I know we're fine today.

Debbie: All right. Well, whenever, I guess.

Jack: All right. In fact, earlier the better, because...

Debbie: Huh?

Jack: I said, try to come earlier the better because my mom is at a meeting.

Debbie: What time is she supposed to be... Is she already gone?

Jack: Yeah.

Debbie: You're positive?

Jack: Yes.

Debbie: All right. Promise?

Jack: Yes.

Debbie: Pinky promise?

Jack: Yes.

Debbie: Say 'pinky promise.'

Jack: Pinky promise.

Debbie: All right. Well tell me a time.

Jack: 10 o'clock.

Debbie: Okay, that sounds good.

Jack: Okay.

Debbie: All right.

Jack: All right.

Debbie: Do you want me to call you around that time?

Jack: Yeah, you can call me.

Debbie: Are you sure? All right.

Jack: All right.

Debbie: All right, bye.

Conversation #6
June 21st ~10:00am

Jack: Hello?

Debbie: Hey.

Jack: Hey.

Debbie: What are you doing?

Jack: Nothing. What are you doing?

Debbie: Driving.

Jack: Oh. Where are you?

Debbie: I'm almost there. Huh?

Jack: I was just asking where you were.

Debbie: Oh, I'm getting ready to turn on (interstate) 75.

Jack: Okay.

Debbie: You're sure everything is clear?

Jack: Yeah, everything's fine.

Debbie: Promise?

Jack: Yeah.

Debbie: All right.

Jack: All right.

Debbie: Okay. Be outside, okay?

Jack: All right.

Debbie: All right, bye.

Jack: Bye.

Debbie envisioned a future with Jack. She delusionally dreamed of living with Jack and telling everyone of their relationship when he turned 18. She planned to follow him to High School by obtaining a teaching position at King High School. She even proposed the idea of marriage to Jack. Her seriousness in pursuing the relationship validates that Debbie didn't view herself as a criminal. She knew that their relationship was wrong and encouraged Jack not to tell anyone, but she was lying to even herself in believing that there was anything genuine in this affair. What she didn't know even more so was that it was this mentality that had intimidated Jack to the point of not wanting to see her anymore. He was not ready for a serious commitment – not at the age of 14 and *especially* not with a teacher, no matter how attractive she was.

As Debbie pulled up, unsuspectingly to Jack's home, she was grateful to have one more day with the man she believed she had strong feelings for. Police officers pulled in front of and behind Debbie's car. Even then she was confused. She had no idea what was going on. An officer approached her car and explained that he needed to take her to the police station to discuss her relationship with Jack Carpenter. Without saying a word, staring blankly at the officer, Debbie nodded slowly.

A detective helped her into the squad car.

AFTER THE ARREST

Immediately after the arrest, Debbie was transported to the local police department. Her heart raced as she thought about what would happen next. Besides a simple speeding ticket, she had never been in trouble with the law. She was not handcuffed, though the stiff, leather police car seats reminded her a doctor's examination table. Debbie was sent to a holding area upon arrival at the station. She was alone, but voices inside the cell haunted her. The room had no windows and the temperature was chilling. Scuffmarks covered the walls. She wondered how many people had tried to escape this claustrophobic abyss. Seconds seemed like hours; minutes, like years.

She refused to sit down. The alternatives to standing were a small concrete bench or the urine soaked floor. The small aluminum toilet appeared to have fecal matter on it that looked as though it had not been cleaned for days. The smell was putrid.

"I do not belong in a place like this," she thought. "I am a college graduate and an educator."

Her arrogance filled her body. She was better, more educated, more intelligent than any others who inhabited this room before her. This room was never designed for someone like her.

After the Arrest

She hadn't really done anything wrong. And yet, as she continued to examine the walls, and continued to be accosted by the putrid stench, the true reality of this situation pressed into her. She pressed her back against the cold, filthy wall, and sank down to the floor. Slowly, all of her thoughts melded into one, "I might be going to jail."

An officer confirmed her worst fear: her arrest had been released to the public and she would now be transported to the Hillsborough County Jail. The media would prove to be Debbie's worst nightmare. Teachers are held to a higher moral standard than most, and when one falls short of these expectations, it seems that the media can always be found lurking in the shadows waiting to break the dark story.

At the jail, Debbie was escorted into booking. The officer directed her to a chair and harshly told her to sit down. To her right sat a heavyset young Spanish man. His clothes, stained with soured alcohol and sweat, permeated into her clothes, her hair, her brain. The more he perspired, the more intense the smell became. Appearing lifeless, the young drunken man slept through his name being called. Not long after, while sitting in a nightmarish daze, Debbie heard her own name. She walked over to the officer who then proceeded to search every inch of her body for weapons or drugs.

Once cleared, she was escorted to central booking. Debbie tried to stare straight-ahead, avoiding eye contact with anyone. She forced herself to go to a place where nothing, and no one, could harm her. This was not the first time in her life she had gone to this place – this dark corner of her mind.

She spoke to a man while waiting to be booked. Her heart was palpitating. She was scared to breathe. A solitary tear painfully seared her cheek. The first lesson she learned in jail was not to cry. Crying equates weakness; weakness shows vulnerability; and vulnerability leads to destruction.

Debbie was called up to be booked. An older guard guided her to the finger printing section. This guard was stern, but polite. Although his eyes were dark, Debbie felt that she saw a glimmer of compassion in them. His face remained virtually emotionless as he took each finger and set them on the computerized machine. Then he took her picture – the picture that would become her infamous mug shot.

Debbie returned to her seat and waited unknowingly. An hour passed when suddenly she heard her name being shouted. She stood up and followed another guard to yet another small room. A glass partition separated her from a man she would learn was her court appointed attorney, John Fitzgibbons. He was an older man with an odd disposition. She didn't know if it was his wrinkled shirt, or his straw-like hat, but something about him made her nervous. She sat patiently in her chair while he fumbled through papers in his well-worn briefcase. He took off his hat, revealing a head of white hair, and looked directly into her eyes.

"You know you are facing 30 years in prison," he stated. Denial reared its ugly head and Debbie stormed out of the glass-encased room.

The meeting adjourned, Debbie was led to a room to change into her jail garb. She was given the same brilliant orange jumpsuit as the other inmates. She quickly changed into the suit and handed her street clothes to the officer in charge. A guard was waiting for her outside of the changing quarters to bring her to a place she will forever remember – solitary confinement.

Better known as, "The Hole." After navigating down several corridors with guards watching her every move, Debbie arrived at this dark, dreary end. She had expected the guards to treat her differently. She was a teacher for God's sake, an educated woman, certainly not some low-life. But in their eyes, Debbie was not different from the girl standing beside her – a hard-core criminal. The guards didn't care if you were black, white, or purple. They were trained in the school of Hard Knocks. Their sole purpose, other than maintaining order, was to make jail time a living nightmare. Debbie's arms wrapped around herself, she held her jail uniform in her hands. The guard motioned her upstairs and she robotically walked up each step to her cell. The eyes of solitary confinement veterans stalked her on her walk of shame.

She walked numbly into her cell. The door slammed and locked behind her. A bed, toilet/sink, leftover filth, and humidity's warm breath were all the comforts offered to her. She proceeded to make her aluminum, tear-stained bed. She crept in and lay on her back, staring at the mold growing on the ceiling. A guard rapping on her door broke her concentration. He demanded she come with her down another seemingly endless hallway to the room where her delusions came to life.

Debbie found herself walking into the examining room of the nurses' station and began to panic. She knew that they were looking for DNA evidence of the sexual act. The examination was "standard procedure" for this type of offense. Debbie shed her jumpsuit and was given a paper-thin gown to wear over her chest. She stood naked from the waist down, and confronted fear after fear, insecurity after insecurity, skeleton after skeleton. Debbie was not a stranger to feeling violated. Her body was sacred to her and to endure this violation again was agonizing. The nurse asked her to lie down on a heavily sanitized aluminum table. Ammonia wafted into her nostrils like poison. The nurse began her examination as Debbie wept tears of pain. She wept for the loss of her innocence, the loss of her life, as she knew it. Endearingly, the nurse asked if she had been raped. Debbie wanted to scream and yell that yes, she *was* raped! Raped of her choices, raped of her heart, raped of her soul, and raped of the life she once had!

At the conclusion of the examination, she redressed in her orange garb and walked zombie-like back to her cell. Debbie could no longer keep the daunting voices and memories at bay. Her mind flooded with malicious thoughts of herself. She didn't want to be this person anymore. She couldn't stand to wake up in the morning in this disgusting room as an inmate. She had been ripped apart from who she thought she was and if she couldn't go back, then she certainly didn't want to go forward. She wanted to end this Debbie's life now. She desperately looked around for something to aid her in her endeavor, but found nothing. She looked at her hands, trembling from the silent rage within. Tears burned her cheeks as they silently rolled down. She took her fingernail and dug it deep into her wrist as hard as she could. Fresh blood began to appear as she pushed down even harder. *Could this actually work?* Just then a guard yelled up to her cell. Debbie quickly doused her wrist with water, and watched the blood flow down the sink. She held her wrist close by her side so no guard could see what she had done. She didn't know where she would go if they found out. After all, she was already in the hole.

Debbie remained in the hole for the night. She tried to sleep, but her own thoughts haunted her, and the piercing screams of the other inmates made her cringe. She was released from jail the next afternoon.

The charges against Debbie were two counts of lewd or

lascivious behavior involving a minor between the ages of 12 and 16. Later, one count of lewd and lascivious exhibition would be added to these existing charges. Warrants were written a few days after her release and authorities searched her townhome.

In a matter of days, hours, Debbie's entire world was shaken. Her face streamed across every news channel. Whispers traveled from ear to ear about the teacher who slept with her student. Though it was summer, as soon as the school district received word of Debbie's arrest, she was placed on administrative duty status and would soon be placed on suspension without pay. Owen, understandingly, took the news the hardest. He drank a lot and often couldn't stand to be near Debbie. His alcoholism and bitterness turned to rage and frustration. He yelled and fought with Debbie often. He called her a whore and despite any mistakes he made during this trying time, he justified them through the statement, "Well, at least I didn't sleep with a 14-year-old." On one occasion even taking her delicate throat into his hands. The two split a few weeks later after Owen filed for divorce, ending their 1 year, 16 day marriage.

Her case went national. She rose to the ranks of Pam Smart and Mary Kay Letourneau. Headlines read "SEX-CHARGED TEACHER WAS NICK CARTER'S HIGH SCHOOL SWEETHEART;" and Debbie was described as "the sexy blonde teacher whose scandalous relationship with a 14 year old student has shocked America." Websites were specifically created and dedicated to Debbie and her case: DebraLafave.com, DebraBeasleyLafave.com, DebraLafave.net, and DebraLafave.org. She became famous nearly overnight. Why did her case in particular stir up so much media attention? The age of the student was certainly eye catching, but more than that, it was Debbie's astounding beauty that captured the continuous gaze of her audience. Sex sells – beauty sells; and Debbie was in no short supply.

Thankfully her family stood by her side, along with her lawyer, John Fitzgibbons. Debbie turned towards God during this time as well. With His support, and the support of her family and legal team, Debbie endured the next several months as best as possible. Evidence continued to be gathered against her. In mid-October it was confirmed that Debbie's DNA was found present in a sample taken from Jack.

Two psychological reports were written during this time. One was completed by the state department, and another was completed privately. These reports ultimately conflicted with one another as the state found that Debbie appeared to be unimpaired at the time of the acts, and the private psychological report showed that Debbie continued to suffer from mental illness. Given the information, it certainly appeared as though insanity was the defense's best option.

A trial date was set for July 18, 2005 – a year following the criminal acts. In that time, Debbie had no contact with Jack or his family. Both attorneys advocated for a plea deal in hopes of avoiding a trial, but could not come to an agreement as Fitzgibbons stated that they would not agree to a plea deal involving prison time. If convicted, Debbie could have faced at least 30 years in a federal prison.

Following a hearing with Circuit Court Judge Wayne Timmerman, during which both attorneys told to be ready to start trial on December 5th, Debbie's attorney made the following infamous statement: "To place an attractive young woman into that kind of hellhole is like putting a piece of raw meat in with the lions. I'm not sure that Debbie would be able to survive." No one wants to go to jail, especially not someone as sweet, gentle, and vulnerable as Debbie. To some, Fitzgibbons' statement meant that no one so beautiful should be placed in a prison. To others, he seemed to be essentially equating a prison sentence to a death sentence.

Media attention resumed with full fervor with the looming trial date fast approaching. The pre-trial had taken a toll on Jack, and his mother grew ever more concerned about the long-term affects of a trial on her son. With tensions continuing to rise, and the possibility of having her son's identity exposed to the media, she made likely one of the most difficult decision she had ever had to make.

On November 22, 2005, both attorneys came before Judge Timmerman and disclosed that a plea deal had been reached. The long standoff between the parties had finally come to an end. Debbie would not be prosecuted, and instead, she plead guilty to the charges and would serve three years of community control (house arrest), and seven years' probation.

Debbie effectively ended her teaching career with her guilty plea; her Florida teaching license was automatically revoked, and no other state will grant a teaching credential to a convicted felon. Under the terms of her probation, she had to be home by 10 pm every day, could not leave Hillsborough County without a judge's permission, and could not be around children. She also had to register as a sex offender.

But Debbie was not out of the clear yet. She still had charges to face in Marion County for the acts in Ocala. On December 8, 2005, Marion County Circuit Judge Hale Stancil rejected the plea deal, claiming that any agreement that didn't require Debbie to serve some prison time "would undermine the credibility of this court, and the criminal justice system as a whole, and would erode public confidence in our schools." He set a trial date for April 10, 2006. The Marion County state's attorney subsequently dropped the charges. In a statement, the prosecutors cited an assessment by psychologist Martin Lazoritz that found the victim would be so severely traumatized by a potential trial that it would take as long as eight years for him to recover. Based on this, prosecutors said that putting LaFave on trial would not be worth the harm to the victim's well-being.

Debra Jean Beasley LaFave never sat before a jury of her peers. I feel like, if I had been a part of that hypothetical jury, the question I ultimately would have wrestled with would have been, "Is this lady seriously a predator, with full knowledge of what she did at each calculating moment, and is guilty? Or, is this woman inherently mentally disturbed and essentially crazy, and is innocent?" Man, that would have been a difficult question. Frankly, I'm quite glad that this is in fact *only* a hypothetical question.

Debbie never said anything to the victim after her crime. She did, however, tell him and his family through the media that she was deeply sorry.

THERAPY

Debbie had been in and out of therapy her entire life. She had pleaded guilty to her crimes to stay out of prison, but believe herself not guilty. After her arrest, Debbie experienced depression, guilt, impulsive behaviors, shame, and even a little bit of excitement due to her notoriety. Not surprisingly, she was mandated to therapy again. Debbie went to a bipolar expert in Cincinnati. Based on this doctor's professional opinion, she advised Debbie's mom to seek help from a local doctor. It was said by both doctors, that Debbie was rapidly cycling and they were concerned that she would slip into a deep depression, and possibly attempt suicide once again.

When she visited the local doctor, he had her do a series of tests based on the symptoms she had at the moment. Debbie's judgment was compromised, so she relied on the professional opinion of her doctor and her mom. He prescribed her a medication called lithium. His reasoning behind this was because the drug quickly reduces rapid cycling and stabilized her mood. Over time, and a close relationship with her doctor, Debbie started to live a somewhat normal life. Debbie began to see Joni, a leader of group therapy for sexual predator rehabilitation, while still having her medication tweaked. One of Joni's orders was to stay on this medication.

Debbie didn't open up right away because she was intimidated by all of the men in the class. Again, data shows that most sexual predators are men. That first session, Debbie walked into a room with several pairs of hungry, male eyes drooling over the breath of femininity that just glided into the room. Not exactly the environment to foster openness from someone who's past was so splattered with bad men. And on top of that, Debbie didn't feel like she belonged in this room at all. During the initial time after her crime, she was very angry with her victim. Victim – Debbie didn't even like using that word for Jack. He had been a willing participant in all of their engagements. After all, he came on to her first. She felt that Jack was just as guilty as she was.

In her therapy, Debbie continued to process all of the events leading up to her arrest. She insisted that the sexual feelings were initiated by the victim. Debbie herself was flattered by the attention he was giving her through casual flirting. She was in a troubled marriage and wasn't feeling very attractive or womanly. It was nice to be noticed and appreciated – even if it was just for her body. She felt more emotionally attracted to her victim that sexually aroused, but she admits that she took advantage of his arousal. She took control; she took on the role of the abuser with this power. She once again used her body to control a man. *But how could a teacher who wanted to make young girls aware of sexual abuse, be - herself - a sexual abuser?* This question constantly swirled in her mind. As their relationship moved from flirting, to kissing, to sex, her victim became more aggressive, sending vivid memories of her rapes and previous abusers to the forefront of her mind. She instinctively drew back, becoming more passive in the relationship. She was familiar with this scenario and began doing whatever he wanted to do. The roles had been reversed. Debbie spoke with her victim like a young girlfriend, not as an adult.

These were the feelings she had leading up to her arrest. She was never sexually turned on by him, but rather was turned on because she felt needy and was not intimidated by her victim. Through several sessions guided by her therapist, Debbie began asking questions of herself. *Why do I always give my body to those who will abandon me in the end?*

Time went on and her class turned out to be one of the only support groups she had. After getting involved in therapy, she realized that she was the adult whether she felt like it or not. She realized that she should have been the one to not cross the line. She felt sorry that Jack and his family had to suffer because of her actions. As part of her therapy, Debbie wrote a letter from the perspective of her victim.

> *Ms. Beasley,*
>
> *I want to say that I don't hate you. I do however blame you for the turmoil in my life over the last 2 years. Although I did consent to sex with you, you should have been the adult in the situation. You should have been able to draw the line between student and teacher. When my mom confronted me about you, I felt very awkward. I didn't want to get you in trouble, but my mom and I had an extremely close relationship. I experienced tremendous guilt when I told her and I was depressed for days. Being a guy, I was supposed to be proud. Right, Ms. Beasley? Well, I wasn't. My friends thought I was a wuss when I "ratted" you out. Ms. Beasley do you know that the media followed me around for months[?] My*

picture was plastered on an international website. You took away my family's privacy. We couldn't even leave the house for the first couple of weeks.

I was raised to be self-sufficient. My dad left when I was little, so I was the only male around the house. I had become afraid to ask for help because I would have to admit that I am weak. So, I immersed all that I felt into basketball. Things eventually got too bad at school. I was being made fun of by the guys and rejected by the girls. My teenage years are all over because of you. You have taken those years away from me. As a result of all of this, me and my family has had to pick up and leave town.

So Ms. Beasley, I don't wish you ill will. I do hope that you have time to realize what you have done to me and my family. With your punishment, you will never be able to exploit another child again.

After a time, Debbie found that she enjoyed therapy very much. It was tremendously beneficial when her mind was on overload, and her doctor could help her sort things out. The instruction and communication in her sessions helped Debbie to realize that she can change her mood based simply on her thought patterns. It forced her to hold herself accountable for her moods. She could no longer blame exterior things on her actions.

She was able to work through several underlying concerns – again with the help of a therapist. I mention this so often because of the stigma often associated with mental illness. There should be no shame in seeking help to work through issues that cannot be resolved on one's own. Debbie was able to work through the lack of affection she received from her father. When she brought home her treatment plan, Larry was offended. He asked her if she felt like he was a bad father. Debbie was able to explain to him that she never felt like he was a bad father, but felt like he didn't give her the affection she so craved. His punishment for those around him when he disapproved or was angry was withdrawal. Debbie wrote her father a letter as well, and this one may have been even more difficult to write. She had been storing these words for him for years, and finally felt confident enough to write them down. She felt guilty the entire time she penned the letter, but knew that these words needed to be written and read if her relationship with her father was ever going to be able to heal.

Dad,

I am not the best communicator and I don't think you are either. So, that is why I am writing a letter to you. Last night really bothered me. First of all, your own daughter died from a drunk driver. How can you justify having Hank drive home, even though he lives 10 blocks away[?] Most accidents happen near home. Look at Angie, she was just about home, and she died, instantly. Not only that, there were cops out all night long.

When I went to ask you about last night, I knew what your reaction would be. But, I thought I would let you know anyway. I understand where you are coming from, I am your daughter and I should respect your wishes. And I do for the most of the time. I know it's hard, but you need to realize that not all things are revolved around sex. I'm sure you think that way considering the crime that I committed. As bad as I feel, I have to try to live my life also. You have a way of making me feel guilty when I do something you don't approve of. You did the same thing with Angie and she died before you could even let her know that you weren't ashamed of what she did. For years, you have enabled me to take what people do to me because I don't want to create an upset. The same way I have reacted to you. This letter may seem harsh, but I am tired of the way you treat me. You are so fake sometimes that I just want to shut you out completely. I don't know what mom and I ever did to you, but somehow we are your enemies. Christmas morning was awesome. I wish you treated us like that all the time, but you don't. It's so hard to respect you when you don't respect either one of us.

I want you to know that I am an adult. A grown woman who now can make rational decisions in my life. If I want a man to stay the night with me, I will. Your rules are too rigid. I am not a child. And though I live under your roof, I am still an adult and I can make my own choices. I am fully aware that you will crawl into your hole and ignore me until I conform back into what you want me to be. My life, our lives, are not normal and I completely take responsibility for it. There is not a day that goes by that I don't wake up feeling ashamed and guilty for what I did to you and mom. But it happened and now I must move forward. I have a job that allows me to pay my bills and a mind that allows me to be somewhat normal now.

I guess what I am trying to say is… A majority of my life has been taken away from me, even if it was my own doing. I am 26 years old. Two years older than Angie was when she died. Let me live my life; don't take any more away from me than what I have already lost. I am dating. It's what people do my age. Just because I date one guy after another, I am not promiscuous. Despite what you may think of me. I am a big girl who can stand up for herself. Finally. So, if I want

Therapy

Hank or anyone else for that matter, to stay over, I will. And I don't have to ask for your permission. I am in a situation that I cannot control right now. If you run me out, know that I can find somewhere else to go. I don't want to do that because I love being here. If you choose to ignore me and give me the cold shoulder, well then that's your own problem. I am no longer going to feel guilty for not living the way you want me to live. Hopefully, you can open your mind, for the first time, and understand where I am coming from. I am my own person and I pay to live where I live. I do not want to disobey you, nor did Angie. But we both hated the way you treated us and I know I will remember it forever. You have enough to work on yourself to be so overly concerned about what I do. I am stable right now and able to make my own rational decisions. She never got to tell you how you made her feel. She died, knowing that her father was disappointed in her. Think about that when you attempt to deal with all that I am telling you. Don't do this to the only child you have left. You are a miserable person who still has so much going for you. Would you please wake up and see that life is about compromising. It's one thing if you don't want to, but to make things a little more civil around this house, work on your issues, not everybody else's.

I know this letter sounds harsh, but it is truly how I feel. I don't have the courage to tell you this face to face. Be there for me not because you have to, because I need your support. I am not a slut or promiscuous. I know you feel that way about me and you may always will. But, I know one thing. I need you to back off with the demanding, controlling father role. If only you could put that much effort into supporting me and making me feel like I mean something to you.

I want to be the grownup that I am. Despite all of the mistakes that I have made, I have recovered quite well. I have a long life ahead of me and I feel like I am on the right track. Please quit being so demanding of me. Let me make my own decisions. For the most of my life I based my decisions on how you and mom would perceive me. I never found myself. I kept falling into a hole until I did something where I couldn't get out. I know you are ashamed of what I did. It affected your image also. I understood you. I have lived with you long enough to know how you think.

So, you have a choice. I am not asking you to hold in your feelings and let them eat you alive. You have got to be able to see you where I am coming from. I am sorry to have to write a letter like this, but it is finally necessary. I can't take it anymore. I love you and I always will. I do respect you, but I need, for my own emotional and mental growth, to make decisions on my own. I don't want to be 26 and still living with my parents. But, that was how the cards were dealt. I need a small amount of freedom. And I need to have a father who is there when times are good and when times are bad. Your presence alone is not enough. It never has been. I have held onto the words in cards and the thoughtful gifts that you have given me. I want you. I have had enough of you making excuses to me and mom. These words come from a lifetime of hurt, guilt, and shame that you have placed on my heart. Please take this letter as something to learn from.

All my love,

Deb

It took Larry some time to absorb the words in his daughter's letter, but he became serious about working on the relationship with his family. Debbie now champions her father as one of her greatest supporters, though he is not perfect. Additionally, Joyce learned from Debbie as well. She learned that her submissiveness toward Larry modeled how to be a victim. She has become a stronger role model for her daughter and the two have grown ever closer throughout the healing process in the years following her arrest. Debbie is grateful for the opportunity to learn from the mistakes of her parents, as well as her own mistakes.

There once was a time when Debbie felt victimized by the men in her life, including her father. She felt as though she was the only one experiencing pain in these relationships. Subconsciously, she allowed each man that came into her life to control her. She had no independence or individuality. Debbie now realizes though that she used this mentality to never blame herself for anything. As a victim, she could always blame the bad things that happened to her on other people, men in particular. She never had to take responsibility for her own life – for her own decisions. But years of insecurity and low self-esteem led to body distortions. The only part of her life she felt she had any control over was her body and her eating. Eating, control, sex – all of these things Debbie realized were connected. Through therapy, she finally was able to take the bull by the horns – so to speak. She continued to work on eating healthy, exercising, and changing her negative thought patterns. There are days when she can't see her psychiatrist, or she doesn't eat healthy, or she isn't able to exercise, but she constantly reminds herself to have positive thoughts about her body and her life. She may always struggle with self-esteem and depression, but Debbie knows that it is worth it to pursue a healthy, balanced body and mind.

Debbie lost her job, her husband, and her life as she knew it; but, she has also gained much more. Debbie was finally able to get the help she needed. She no longer lives with spirals of emotions. She still has issues from her past, and often her therapist forces her to go back there in order to deal with things that she had swept under the rug for many years. Writing and reading have helped her the most during treatment. Writing has given her a healthy outlet to express herself. Reading has educated her on her illness. There were so many things she didn't understand about being bipolar. Now when she reads the passages that may seem far-fetched to most, she understands them and it lets her know that she is not alone.

She wishes she hadn't had sex with a minor. She wishes that she hadn't hurt so many people that she loved. But these are things she cannot change. She believes that she committed this sex crime because she wanted to have power in the situation that felt so similar to her adolescent rape. There was no conscious thought, "I am going to have sex with a minor in order to feel like I am in control." It was only through therapy that she has been able to come to this conclusion. Debbie had been submissive in every relationship after her rape. She felt powerless – like she had no voice of her own to speak with and speak for. When her victim came along, he reminded her so much of the boy who sexually assaulted her.

She can't say that great things come out of committing a crime and being arrested; she doesn't like what she did and she will never do it again. But she is a different person, a better person today. Debbie is now a person who feels secure in herself. She has learned how to stand up for herself, an issue she had dealt with her entire life. She had taken things lying down for so many years. She would allow other people to make decisions

Therapy

for her, allowing them to walk all over her. She was isolated and often times felt alone, sulking in pity party after pity party. She never took responsibility for those actions, but blamed others for making her feel and act that way. She is no longer afraid to challenge herself. The little girl sitting in the corner by herself no longer exists. For the first time, she feels behind the wheel of life. She now feels capable of taking charge, though she still works on being assertive rather than aggressive. With new medication that specifically targets her mental health needs, and a new support system, Debbie continues to make great progress.

EPILOGUE: LIFE EVER AFTER

I sincerely hope that this book gives light and insight into the life and person of Debbie. So much can be assumed and perceived through very little information, and I feel that many people who have heard of Debbie and her story, judge her based off of a small period in her life. There are trying periods in each of our lives that are less than shining, and isn't it how we emerge from these trials that truly defines us?

Over a decade has passed since Debra LaFave became a household name, and in that time much has changed for Debbie. She is a simple person, and enjoys her calm, slow-paced life. She doesn't like the spotlight. She shops at yard sales and consignment shops. She doesn't think high and mighty of herself. Debbie is still a stunningly beautiful person, though I don't know if she thinks of herself like that. She rarely wears makeup and really doesn't need it. She continues to be a good friend, though we do go through periods without contact. Debbie and I got really close after my mom, Maria G. Zuniga, passed away. She was there when I needed her and we got to spend a lot of time together. I attended her children's birthday party and her

Epilogue: Life Ever After

and her mom attended my family's birthday parties and baby showers. My family accepted them with open arms and invited them to all family occasions like parties, weddings, and quinceñeras. My family knew about Debbie's past and didn't judge her, instead accepted her, protected, and defended her because they seen the goodness in her heart.

Both Debbie's parents are still alive and living in Ruskin. Debbie is still very close with her mom. I had the pleasure of meeting both Larry and Joyce. Larry is very laid-back, and loves to go shooting. Joyce is always polite, and welcomed me into her home. However, I felt that she never truly approved of me and my close relationship with Debbie. I could not think of the reason why but I remember that Debbie once told me her mother used to have racial prejudices. During one visit, Debbie mentioned those past racial prejudices to me in front of her mother, and Joyce lost all words. Joyce explained that the times were different back then and that she no longer felt that way. I believed her of course!

Debbie now works at a butterfly farm. The butterflies float through the air and warm her heart. She feels comforted by the butterflies, like Angie is close to her. Debbie also has two beautiful, young boys whom she loves dearly. Their father is Shawn Haverfield. Though they are not married, the two do live together with the boys. Debbie is a great parent. She is very much involved in all aspects of their lives and does a lot with her kids. She tries daily to give her children the love, affection, and attention she so craved as a young girl. If her children come up to her while she is engaged in conversation, she will disengage and give them their full attention. Debbie is not without her qualms, however. She continues to struggle with germs, and cannot live without hand sanitizer. This likely stems from some persistent control issues. She's very cautious when is comes to her children. She is into essential oils and makes her own remedies, especially for the boys if they are sick. Debbie would like to have more children with the right person.

I think of all that I admire most about Debbie, her voice and love of music touch my heart in ways that are nearly indescribable. Music is love to Debbie. Though she doesn't sing professionally anymore, I distinctly remember the first time I was moved by her angelic voice. It was a lazy afternoon, and Cris, my nephews Cristopher and Aaliyah and I were at Debbie's house. Cristopher broke out his guitar and started playing around. Cris asked me to sing the song I had been working on, a country song titled "On this side of the door." Debbie closed her eyes and swayed with the music. She started humming and singing harmonies to my melody. I was astounded! She has a magnificent voice – soft and breathy, but hauntingly beautiful. I couldn't help but stop and compliment her. She giggled, and then told me the story about having a record deal and dating Nick Carter.

"We should record this song together!" I exclaimed enthusiastically.

Debbie was bashful at first, but ultimately decided that it would be a fun thing to do. We recorded the single "On this side of the door" together and I am planning on releasing it soon. Her voice adds another level of depth and intimacy to the track.

Mental health concerns continue to plague Debbie. She's not currently in counseling, but has seen a neurologist. A brain tumor was discovered and based on its size, it is likely that the tumor was present during the scandal in 2004. It's possible that this could also have influenced her behavior and decisions. That is the opinion of the medical professional with which she has

Epilogue: Life Ever After

been consulting. Stress and anxiety are ever present in her daily life. She gets overexcited, almost to the point of hysteria. There are times when Debbie becomes overwhelmingly involved or supportive of a cause or idea, only to completely leave it behind a short time later. This also goes for people. Sometimes she just can't be bothered, which explains the absence of her friendship for several weeks at a time. With those whom she loves and trusts though, she typically comes back around after these episodes pass.

The affects of her past mistakes continue to haunt her. Debbie continues to have financial difficulties as she has a hard time getting a job. She is still registered as a sex offender. She has to go to the police office station every month to check in and let them know that she is still living in her current residency. People are still ugly to her. It doesn't matter that she has never again been convicted of a crime as a sexual offender. People remember her in infamy and many are hateful towards her. She is still often contacted by random people. In one instance, Debbie and my sister Cris were having lunch at a local establishment and a few women in the restaurant recognized her. Cris didn't realize at the time what was happening, but Debbie did. After they ate their lunch and were back in the car, Debbie told Cris about the women. She stated that she overheard one of the women say something ugly about her. She brushed it off casually, but Cris was furious. Cris wished she had had the opportunity to say something to that woman. Knowing that Cris would be very protective of her, Debbie preferred to avoid the whole situation by not telling her till after they left.

Yes, Debbie made some mistakes, but she has also made significant progress in the years after. And shouldn't we be encouraging that? Rehabilitation? How is someone ever expected to grow and learn and change if we are constantly bombarding him or her with the labels of what *we* think that they are? Hate breeds hate. It cannot change anything to make it good again. I believe in second chances and that no one person is better than another.

Each person should be treated with respect and dignity. We all have a duty as human beings to help each other to grow and flourish. That's the only way we can survive together. We must support each other and learn to recognize the beauty within. Debbie created a small life, all on her own. It may not be perfect, but it's hers. She has overcome many obstacles and has gone through some amazing transformations over her lifetime. And isn't it fitting then, how similar her story is to the one symbol she holds most dear – that of a beautiful butterfly? Delicate and carefree, it floats through life bringing joy to those around it. You would never know the struggles it took and the journey it made to get to where it is today. Be blessed!

ABOUT THE AUTHOR

Joe Zuniga was born in Miami, Florida and currently lives in Ruskin, a small town 20 miles south of Tampa, Florida. He's the product of a single mother with a Christian upbringing. Joe and his family were migrants that traveled throughout the country working in the fields, picking vegetables and fruits. He lived in government housing and attended a Head Start program through the Redlands Christian Migrant Association as a child.

As a teenager, Joe discovered a love for music and learned to play different instruments. He pursued music and aspired to become a recording artist; however, peer pressure and temptation led him towards the wrong crowd, and Joe eventually landed in prison. After completing 5 years in prison and 4 years supervised release, Joe decided to make major changes in life. After prison, Joe received a degree in business, studied business in Europe, and launched his company Zuniga Marketing, Inc. Unfortunately, during this time, his mother's health drastically deteriorated so Joe became her primary care taker as well.

In 2011, Joe realized his adolescent dreams and decided to professionally launch his singing career. In 2012, Joe became the first in Florida to be nominated for a Tejano Music Award and also won a Tejano Globe Award for his first single, "Atado A Tu Amor". Joe was also a finalist on the international Latino talent show Tengo Talento Mucho Talento. Since then, Joe has traveled and performed at various venues throughout the country.

Joe's mother passed away on New Year's 2015. She inspired him to tell his story and help others. Joe now performs his music and shares his powerful story in a unique, entertaining, and inspirational way at every memorable event. In addition to sharing his own unique story, he hopes to be a voice through which others can share their stories.

CPSIA information can be obtained
at www.ICGtesting.com
Printed in the USA
BVHW072052150722
642052BV00005B/697